CAPTAIN OF THE

Ship

A Book on Living an Exciting and
Unusual Success-Filled Life

MARK MONTANUS

BALBOA.
PRESS

A DIVISION OF HAY HOUSE

Balboa Press books may be ordered through booksellers or by contacting:

Balboa Press
A Division of Hay House
1663 Liberty Drive
Bloomington, IN 47403
www.balboapress.com
1 (877) 407-4847

Because of the dynamic nature of the Internet, any web addresses or links contained in this book may have changed since publication and may no longer be valid. The views expressed in this work are solely those of the author and do not necessarily reflect the views of the publisher, and the publisher hereby disclaims any responsibility for them.

The author of this book does not dispense medical advice or prescribe the use of any technique as a form of treatment for physical, emotional, or medical problems without the advice of a physician, either directly or indirectly. The intent of the author is only to offer information of a general nature to help you in your quest for emotional and spiritual well-being. In the event you use any of the information in this book for yourself, which is your constitutional right, the author and the publisher assume no responsibility for your actions.

Any people depicted in stock imagery provided by Thinkstock are models,
and such images are being used for illustrative purposes only.
Certain stock imagery © Thinkstock.

ISBN: 978-1-5043-7251-0 (sc)
ISBN: 978-1-5043-7283-1 (e)

Print information available on the last page.

Balboa Press rev. date: 01/27/2017

ACKNOWLEDGEMENTS

The author would be in remiss if he did not identify and say thank you to the friends and colleagues who assisted in the development of this book.

Thanks to an old friend Dick Huesby for critiquing much of the writing. Thanks to certified nutritionist Rachel Goodwin for providing her expertise in the writing of the chapter on healthy eating. Thanks to Mark Foshee a talented friend and author who provided expertise in helping find the many websites that were used to verify the data presented in the book. His library and computer expertise were critical to the completion of the work. Thanks to my retired Kodak photographer brother, Neil Montanus, for the photo of my boat to be used for the book cover. Many thanks to my wife Charlotte for all of the editing help, for providing ideas in the writing process and for her constant support in the writing process. And last, thanks to my eight children, their spouses and my many grand and great-grand children for supporting me in my work.

Mark Montanus

PREFACE

The captain and his crew sail out to sea not knowing when a storm might hit or the doldrums set in. They will not know of other boats that may cross their path or the location of ice bergs in the north. They will depend upon maps to show the likely areas of danger, but maps will also show the way. The ship will not arrive unless the captain studies the maps and directs the crew to properly set the helm and the sails throughout the entire voyage.

And so it is with you—*Captain of the Ship*. Your life will be faced with all kinds of peril, and, unless you take full responsibility, the trip will be fraught with all manner of difficulty. Study the maps included in this book to navigate through the myriad of experiences that you will encounter in this life. Just as the captain must be knowledgeable, skillful, aware, and dependable, so must you. Set your sails now and take charge of the helm.

The ideas presented here are the maps to help you travel the great and exciting journey.

Good luck Captain!

CONTENTS

Chapter One..1

Where is My Utopia 1

    In the Beginning..1

    Some of the Pitfalls 2

    Independence—The First Magic Word..4

    Responsibility—The Second Magic Word 6

    A Deeper Look at Responsibility 7

    Avoiding Responsibility 8

    The Third Magic Word—Commitment 10

    Ready for the World..11

    Websites on Being Responsible 12

Chapter Two 13

Financial Responsibility 13

    What responsibilities do I face?..13

    Ability to Save and Invest Dollars 14

    What is Compounding..16

    Dollar Averaging 18

    Basic Investing Knowledge and Terminology..................................19

    General Rules for Long-Term Investing 20

    P/E Ratio and Yield..22

    Income vs Growth Stock 23

    Reviewing Your Budget to Start Investing 24

    Honest Budgeting..24

    Expenses Balance 29

    Summary of the Action 32

    The Bank Account 33

    Accounting for the Various Investment Funds 34

    Making Your First Investment..35

    Life Insurance 35

    The Nature of Life Insurance..37

    Buying Your Home 38

    The Final Word 40

    Epilogue..40

    Websites on Financial Success..41

Chapter Three 42

Physical Health—Eating Right 42

    A New Approach to Diet...42

    A Perspective 43

    Personal Diet 43

    Kidney Failure 44

    Understanding the System..45

    Food Label Evaluation Tool..46

    Calories..46

    Salt...46

    Sugar 48

    Potassium...49

    Calcium 49

    Phosphorus 50

    Understanding Food Groups...51

    Animal Meat 52

    Sea Food 53

    Beans, Nuts, and Other Choices 54

    Helpful Hints in Choosing Proteins 54

    Protein Summary 55

    Carbohydrates 56

    Complex Carbohydrates 56

    Carbohydrate Intake 57

    Dietary Fiber 57

    Fats 58

    Cholesterol 60

    Vitamins 61

    Putting it All Together...61

    Finding Healthier Foods 61

    Your Complete Food List 62

    Starting Your New Eating Program 62

Final Thought 63

Food Label Evaluation Tools...64

    Section 1 - Daily Caloric Intake 64

    Section 2 - Content of Salt Sugar Potassium Calcium and Phosphorus-Your Pantry 64

    Section 2A - Searching Store Products...66

    Section 3 – Protein Table 68

    Section 4 – Carbohydrate Table 70

    Section 5 – Fat Table...72

Meal Planning 74
    Breakfast Meals - Section 1 74
    Lunch Meals – Section 2 75
    Dinner Meals – Section 3 76
Additional Nutrition Studies 77
    Nutrition Websites 77

Chapter Four 78
Fitness through Exercise 78
    Are you willing to take on this responsibility? 80
    Aerobic Exercise 80
    Fitness at Home 81
    Exercise—Home or the Gym 82
    Aerobic Fitness in the Gym 83
    What is Strength Training? 83
    Warm-up and cool-down stretches 84
    Anaerobic Fitness at the Gym 84
    Final Notes 84
    Assignment 85
    Websites on Physical Fitness 85

Chapter Five 86
Keeping Mentally Strong 86
    Summary on Innovation 89
    Curiosity 90
    Appreciation 92
    Perspective 92
    Life-Long Learning 94
    Becoming and Staying Mentally Strong 95
    Websites for Further Study 95

Chapter Six 97
Seeking a Spiritual Life 97
    Organized Religion 97
    Meditation and Prayer 99
    Websites to Help in Your Spiritual Journey 101

CHAPTER ONE

Where is My Utopia

We live in this beautiful world where opportunity and abundance exists for all. Wouldn't it be great if you had everything that you need, with a loving wife/husband, happy, growing children, all provided for by a dream job that paid well and was the object of your passion? How nice it would be to have good health, with ample financial resources, with a great feeling about yourself. Seems like utopia, doesn't it? How close are you to this utopia?

Strange, that we live with the possibility of a truly fulfilled life, yet only a small number are able to fully accomplish it. We experience bits and pieces of this utopia, but the greater success seems to escape us, and for some there is only misery. Opportunities are plentiful but so are the pitfalls. *What gets in your way*?

The purpose of this book is to help you understand and overcome *what gets in your way*. So much information is available to help people find their way through the maze of decision making to live a better life. In fact, this material comes at us from all directions and as we study and try to understand, confusion results. It is this author's premise that the majority of self-help books are overwhelming which makes it hard to focus. Much written material will provide recipes and guidelines on how to do it right and most folks can make that work for a while, but success soon fades. Why?

The truth is there are three words that must become part and parcel of your very being in order to find ultimate success. Without any one of them, you cannot achieve a balanced, successful life. In this book, we will take these three magic words and weave them into your psyche until they become part and parcel of who you really are. At that point, you will be able to overcome any obstacle and become what you want to become. You will find your utopia!

In the Beginning

We are born quite helpless and dependent upon someone taking full care of us. The newborn can solicit attention by crying to let others know of his/her needs, but that's about it. So the process begins at zero for the baby. From that point on, there is a steady development that will take the baby from zero ability to care for herself/himself to full growth and independence. By independence, we generally mean that a person is free from the societal pressures that might direct his life. This wonderful process, provided by society, has developed the various structures and systems to help people reach maturity. We are not so much interested in how this maturity process works, as most of the people reading this have supposedly reached maturity, and by society's definition should be able to provide for their own care. The real question is, are most people successful in this process, each fully capable of providing for themselves? As one looks, reads, listens, or watches the news, or just looks around a bit in their own community, one might suspect that a large segment of our society is having difficulty in taking such care.

As we examine the everyday issues that each person faces, two in particular stand out. The first is the issue of personal health. Improper eating habits and lack of exercise are taking an awful toll on society. The obesity problem alone affects over one-third of our society and renders many to an almost helpless state. One can hardly gain independence with such a health problem. Another issue has to do with people's ability to live a sound financial life. It is estimated that about one-third of our society has very little investments and less than $1,000 in the bank. This means that so many live from paycheck to paycheck, completely unable to face problems such as a job layoff or the inability to pay off a large credit card balance. This hardly represents independence.

While health or fiscal problems can easily render a person helpless, our society presents very little opportunity for people to master the understanding and the skill necessary for success. If you find yourself with problems that have kept you from gaining your independence, it is not too late. This book is designed to gird you with the understanding and skills needed for you to become an independent person.

Some of the Pitfalls

The single largest pitfall is that of becoming conditioned by messages from advertisers and others who would like you to do whatever they ask of you. *Keeping up with the Jones* is the perfect example. Advertising has convinced us to become unhappy with what we have, especially if the Jones family next door has a better one. In fact, advertising is very successful in building planned obsolescence into products which causes you to become unhappy with what you bought and encourages you to rush out and buy the latest model. We even anticipate the creation of the latest fashion, then rush out and buy even though what we already have serves perfectly well.

Advertisers are so successful that our country has developed the *more* syndrome. Once we get something, because of advertising messages, we soon long for something better, more toys, more salary, bigger house, fancier car, more stuff—even though what we have serves perfectly well. Is more really better? No, the *more* syndrome will always lead to being unhappy. More is not the answer—we are in this vicious circle of never being satisfied with what we already have. Your *independence* has been stolen from you as you respond to the conditioning of the commercial world. You must be completely able to walk away from these constant messages so that you can make intelligent, informed decisions. This will only happen when you become this special, independent person.

Another pitfall is called the *tribe mentality*. All of us pass through the *tribe mentality* stages quite naturally as we grow up. There are all kinds of social groups such as family, school, scouts, clubs, athletic teams, church, family groups, etc. These are all good institutions and help us to mature. Each group has its own set of rules designed to help each of us function effectively in the group. We pass into certain groups at various stages and out and into another, serving many positive functions.

The tribe (group) has many rules and expects you to abide by them if you want to keep their favor. Take teenagers for example; once that group has decided upon a certain fashion, it immediately becomes something all of them must have in order to be a real member of the tribe. The item may cost too much or a teenager may already have a similar one, but the tribe will be relentless if a teen doesn't have it. While raising eight children, this author often heard the argument, "but Dad, everybody has one."

There are also groups that create a totally negative picture for their members. Street gangs in the inner city become powerful organizations, creating much havoc. Gangs have all kinds of secret rules and everyone in the gang must absolutely respond to what it asks them to do. Once in a gang, it's nearly impossible to get out. Fraternities and sororities in our universities have many activities that are somewhat secret and members must conform to their many rules. Some organizations are fine but some are not. We've often heard of fraternities that are shut down by the University for drinking binges or for conducting harmful and dangerous hazing activities. Many of these organizations can become addicting and gain powerful control over a person's behavior . They can rob you of your independence.

We all remain somewhat tribal for our entire lives just by belonging to a family, joining an activity club, your church, or other useful organization. So where is the danger in the tribal activity? Clearly, belonging to a gang or any group which would result in a negative thing for society should be taboo.

The real danger comes when individuals want so badly to be accepted by a special group that they may do anything that the group asks them to do just to remain in favor with the group. When you are asked to perform something for the group that is against your better judgment, what would you do? You would be surprised how many would acquiesce to the group and give up the commitment to their personal *independence*. You must become your own advocate and develop the responsibility to say "*no*" to a group when you fully know that is not the right thing to do.

This will take some practice on your part as you must become fully aware of the right thing to do when a decision must be made, then do it. That requires you to become an independent person.

Independence—The First Magic Word

The first of three life-changing words is *independence*. To maintain the capability for making choices is a major key. Think of it, a mind thoroughly conditioned by foolish worldly ideas will always keep you dissatisfied and in trouble. Maintaining your independence will point you to a clear pathway allowing you to make smart decisions to help you find success. You will be in control, not some foolish desire resulting from worldly conditioning.

Now, the real question: how do I take back my independence and avoid the powerful influences of constant worldly conditioning? The answer is simple to say but not so easy to do. First, let us seek a broader perspective on the problem.

It begins with the understanding of the difference between wants and needs. A need is something that you must have in order to function properly as a person. That is, when your needs are fully met, you will be able to function properly. Maslow has presented his ideas of moving from basic needs to a hierarchy of needs to wants. In other words, you should provide for food and shelter before thinking about acquiring a motor boat. That is clear enough, but the problem comes when the difference between wants and needs begin to fuzz together. Even a basic need such as transportation is often confused. Buying an automobile can mean A through Z. Where A is buying a vehicle that will allow you to go where you must go safely, comfortably, and economically. Z is buying a vehicle that is very sporty, will go from 0 to 60 in 4 seconds and is something that will make you so happy, momentarily. The problem is that the Z automobile is a gas hog, expensive to purchase and maintain, and not functional for a family of four.

The same can be said of any needs that we are trying to satisfy. Buying more than one needs is a common ailment. When the newness of the thing that you bought wears off, you will become dissatisfied. Not only that, but spending the extra money disallows you from providing some of your other basic needs like insurance, healthy food, or adequate clothing. That will also make you unhappy. What will make you happy? Certainly, it has much to do with being satisfied with who you are and what you already have. Do you really think that you can be happy with a new toy when you do not appreciate what you already have?

First, examine those things which are your basic needs.

Determine where you may have confused wants with needs.

This often happens with transportation and clothing needs. Many have the latest model with all the frills? Designer clothing is often twice as expensive as the non-designer stuff which does the same thing as the expensive model.

Let me tell you a story that happened many years ago. I had graduated from college, gotten married and started my first teaching job. We were able to wisely buy a lovely starter family home which fit our *need*. Of course all of my neighbors had very nice automobiles, so my purchase was a fancy 88 Oldsmobile with all of the bells and whistles. While confusing my wants with my needs, I forgot to include higher insurance and maintenance costs and was disappointed that 20% of our income went to transportation.

Our home was only two blocks from school so I walked to work and the food market was only four blocks away so we often walked there also. It became apparent to me that the Oldsmobile was a definite overkill, so after careful planning, I sold the Olds which did away with high monthly payments that gave me enough cash to buy a 10 year-old Chrysler, with low mileage and was a very stable car.

The Chrysler served us very well for four years and during that time I invested the $100.00 a month, the cost of the Olds, into some very nice stocks. The net result—I felt good about myself that I could rise above the peer pressure and keep my independence. Soon I had more than enough money to buy a little nicer used car where there would be no monthly payments. Since that time, I have carefully chosen to buy things based upon the real need, satisfying this wants thing only when I could afford it and knew that it was important.

The net result for me was a great lesson that I still employ today, 50 years later. I am more than satisfied with everything I have, and I still feel really good about being able to keep my independence all of those years.

1. With a pencil and paper, take the time to review all of those things where you may have confused the wants and needs. This will include all of the things that you currently own, and activities in which you are engaged. That might include eating out, hobbies, attending concerts and events, travel, recreation, etc. Write them down now.

2. Select one of those things that you know is a great offender. It doesn't mean that you must give it up, rather try to find a way to meet the basic need and do away with the expensive wants. If you dine out a lot, you may decide to change the frequency or even find a reasonable substitute. In the case of fast foods, you may want to scrap it for the sake of budget and good health. Make your list now and decide on one that you know you should change. Take the one change and immediately execute the plan. Do it now. Jump to the next step only when you have made a change of one thing successfully. If the change is a large one such as trade for an auto that fits your *need*, it may take some time. If the change is in one of your routine activities such as eating out, it can be implemented immediately, once you have the plan. Stick with the plan religiously.

3. If you are successful with Step 2, you will begin to feel better immediately. Select another item from your list and go to work to meet the basic need and scrap the want. Do it! Continue on with the rest of your list being relentless in understanding your need. If the wants creep in, evaluate their urgency, their cost, net result over the life of the thing being acquired.

"What will the net result be if I am successful?" The most important thing is that you are reclaiming your independence. You become the one that determines your ultimate destiny in every decision. As you meet success with your changes, you will start to feel very good about yourself and the changes that you are making. Because your choices are made as an independent person, you will free yourself from the *more* syndrome. It will make no difference if you neighbor has something better than you. You are fully satisfied with who you are, with what you have, and how you are living your life. Think of it! Your bank account will grow and your health will improve—what a great start

Remember—Independence means that you are the captain of your ship. You are learning to assess the pressures from society and make conscious, thoughtful decisions regarding every opportunity that you meet. You already have the capability to make right decisions. You've proven that by completing the three steps to assess needs and wants and actually changing things for the better.

Welcome to the *success club*. Fully accepting your independence and having exercised it, you are off to a great start—*NEVER LET GO!* Exercise it always, in every decision for the rest of your life.

Responsibility—The Second Magic Word

We must begin by first understanding the nature of being responsible, for it is by taking responsibility of various matters in our lives that we become truly successful. A typical dictionary defines responsibility as a position of being in charge of something. The state or job of being in charge of someone or something and of making sure that what they do or what happens to them is right or satisfactory. This definition goes beyond self and suggests that we must take responsibility for other things or other people. We have two issues here. Number one is that we must be responsible for ourselves to remain fit enough so as to care for all of our needs satisfactorily. We also must be responsible for any obligation that is under our charge such as family. Let us peek at the requirements for accomplishing the first task--that of taking full charge of our own well-being.

The simple truth is the only pathway to a successful life is to take full responsibility for all that you do to become this special, independent person. Without it, you will spend your life wallowing in failure or minimal success.

The logic is self-evident. One can only solve a problem by facing it; however, we are prone to blame other people or circumstances for what goes wrong. You cannot possibly solve your problems if you don't know what they are and are unwilling to face up to your self-created problems.

It all begins with an intense desire to take full responsibility for all of the issues facing your life. This must become and continue to be the underlying motive for your life. You really owe it to yourself and to those who are still taking the responsibility of caring for your inadequacies. Wouldn't it be great if you were in perfect health, with adequate savings and investments to cover any possible problem, if you had a great job resulting from your training and education, you were surrounded by many friends, and were gifted with a spouse and lovely family? Decide to take full responsibility for your life now and get all that you need. The commitment to becoming responsible must now take first priority. If you make the commitment to become responsible, this book will help you get started on an exciting journey that will change your life to a happy, independent, and responsible person, able to weather any storm.

A Deeper Look at Responsibility

To be fully responsible covers more territory than most people understand. Many of you have probably had successes in your life and are working to improve. First, let's take a look at the amazing breadth that may be required of you to gain a full perspective.

Earning power must be adequate to meet all of your current needs and to build savings, contingency, and retirement accounts. Also earning power grows as the family grows.

One's profession must be personally rewarding and provide motivation into higher levels of accomplishment.

Insurance is needed to cover auto, home, life, health, disability and perhaps, even more, according to your lifestyle.

Building equity and maintaining your residence is a prime goal. This includes never adding any unneeded costs to a mortgage loan and paying off the loan in the shortest amount of time possible.

Sound budgeting of your income and expenses is a crucial component. You must at all times remain fiscally solvent, with steady growth in the family assets while maintaining minimal debt.

Good physical health is an absolute requirement so that you can provide continuous care for those who depend on you. This includes physical exercise and healthy eating.

Sound mental health is absolutely required so that your leadership skills can guide you and your family through the many challenges.

Continuing education must be sought after to improve your various skills.

Spiritual values should be sought after by you and your family in order to begin thinking outside of yourself.

Making time in your family routine to be together makes the family stronger.

Preparing the children for college includes a proper mindset and fiscal support.

Provide support for your family as they engage in extracurricular activities. There must be strong encouragement and support for them to succeed.

I am not trying to write a treatise on family living. The above ideas are presented to help you get a complete perspective of the various responsibilities that you will face during your lifetime. The challenges appear formidable. You have no choice, for you will face most of these challenges whether you want to or not. Why not take charge and become fully responsible?

The goal here is to help you develop a wide perspective of the challenges and to see them as wonderful opportunities to serve yourself and others in a very successful and exciting way. Be able to see each of these challenges as events that make your life exciting and worthwhile. More than that, you need to accept full responsibility and take all of these challenges to the highest level possible—always focusing on the development of great human values for you and your family. Your life will be filled with rewards—I guarantee it!

Avoiding Responsibility

Our society seems to have a built in unwillingness to take responsibility for the things in our lives. One of the difficult jobs for a teacher is to help students understand why they are not being successful in their classes. Invariably students attribute failure to things like, the textbook is no good, the teacher is boring, I don't have enough time, and so on. I always treaded lightly on this problem so as not to discourage the student, but it was clear in most cases, that those students did not complete their homework, missed too many classes, or were too busy with a social life. People have a hard time biting the bullet, and they don't want to be blamed for their own failure.

If you talk with almost anyone who has erred, you find that they want to avoid personal responsibility in the matter and blame someone or something else. When that happens, it is very difficult to solve the problem caused by the error because they are not willing to face the truth. Thus, the problem never gets fixed. This has very likely been a problem for you, as most of us have used lame excuses when things didn't work out. It is so easy to blame someone or something else.

It is time now to stop and think hard about this. When something does not go right for you, start with a willingness to look for the error within yourself, in a very honest manner (don't worry about the ego), review every step that you took and you may or may not discover the problem. As the next possible step, talk with a coworker, friend or someone who might understand what you were trying to do. Be very honest with your part. Someone's objective view might discover the problem. If you caused the problem, don't be upset, as every person on earth is open to error. Say thanks, fix the problem, and succeed.

One of my college freshmen students came to my office perplexed because he could not understand the material in a financial accounting course. He said that he put in plenty of study time. After visiting a while, I handed him a weekly calendar where he could record the day and hours he studied last week, with the caveat that he must be absolutely truthful. The paper came back showing 3 ½ hours of study time during the week. I realized then that he was fresh out of high school and as bright as he was, found that an hour or two or sometimes no study at all for his high school classes was usually sufficient. Once he came to realize that to master professional level work would require 8 to 10 hours minimum per week, he was surprised. He responded, did the homework, and had a very successful experience.

From now on, promise yourself that you will be like this student—undaunted by the fact that he was the problem, he tightened his belt and accepted full responsibility and gained much success.

The next paragraph contains a *creed* that must become part and parcel of your life. Read it every day until it becomes an automatic part of you.

> I will assure good health through proper diet and exercise.
> I will assure financial stability by budgeting and making wise use of my assets.
> I will take full responsibility for raising my family in a healthy and positive manner.
> I will take full responsibility for maintaining a good relationship with all of the people in my life.
> I will take full responsibility to improve my talents by continued study, practice, and learning.
> I will take the responsibility to search after the questions regarding our existence and the very nature of being.
> I will take full responsibility for all things that occur in my life.

You can memorize this creed or read it every day until it becomes infused in your entire being, both in your mind and in your heart.

Taking full responsibility must now become a lifetime activity. In every facet of your life, you must be able to evaluate the issues you are facing and make good and thoughtful choices in order to accomplish the highest levels of success. Decide now, at this moment, that you will become truly responsible for yourself and any people under your care.

Congratulations, you have joined the responsible group. Your life will flourish!

The Third Magic Word—Commitment

It seems that western society has difficulty making the ultimate commitment to what it believes. Take new-year resolutions, for example. We no more than make them, then turn right around and ask the question, *which ones are we likely to keep?* This is simply a case of no commitment at all. I'm afraid that society in general does exactly the same with many similar activities. If you continue in this fashion, you could not possibly become this special, responsible, independent person. You have already made your commitment to become this special person, never let it go! The ability to commit must also become part and parcel of your very being. How do you think your family, friends, and coworkers would feel about you if they could always depend upon you? Besides satisfying them, you will accomplish what you set out to do—great. It is as simple as that!

The term commitment can be thought of as *a promise to do something in the future*.

When employers hire, they first look at one's skill and ability to do tasks they will be required to do. A close second for the employer to determine is how committed will this person be to his work and the goals of the company? Employers realize that the most skilled people are not likely to be successful if they are not fully committed to their responsibilities. Would your ability to make a commitment cause you to lose or get the job? Regardless of your answer to the above question, decide now—this very moment, to honor every promise that you will ever make.

The commitment often fails when trying to overcome a problem becomes extremely difficult. Don't give up, keep plugging away and you will overcome the problem. When that happens, you will find that you are extremely pleased with yourself. People find this very difficult to do, in reality it is relatively easy. It does not require mastering difficult concepts or painful hard work. It simply means that you decide once and for all, without any question, to complete what you start to the best of your ability. Even if it is taxing and frustrating.

During my many visits with students of all ages, I was always intrigued by people who were able to quit a frightful habit. This included smoking, drinking to excess, obesity, living a totally sedentary life without exercise, etc. Most who quit their habit successfully took many months and sometimes years to get rid of the habit. A few quit because they came close to a catastrophe. It was always clear to me that those people who took so long to quit, never really made the commitment to quit. "I think I want to quit so I'll try a smokers patch to see if it works." Another would say, "I'll try this diet to see if it works." Those folks were never making any commitment at all to stopping the habit. They were really looking for ways to continue with a close substitute.

Of the people who were perfectly successful, around 20%, not one looked for a substitute; they simply *decided to quit*, once and for all—never looking back, and it was done. Surprisingly, they found it easy to quit. Why, because they *decided* to quit in a complete and total manner. Once done, no further thought was given to it. Only the idea of a complete severing of the habit will allow a *complete* dismissal of the problem.

If you do this and still have pangs of desire, just simply acknowledge the thought then immediately dismiss it from your mind. A few times of doing that successfully and the desire will ultimately go away.

So here you are facing the issue of *total commitment*—but now you have a head start. You now have a much better understanding about what it means for you to become an *independent* person and how to do it. You also have accepted the idea of taking complete responsibility for *everything* in your life. With these two attributes as part of you, it will be much easier for you to become one of the 20%--those who could accomplish something very difficult, with ease.

There are only two rules for you to follow:

> Keep all of the promises that you make to yourself or to anyone else—religiously.
> Be totally honest in all that you say and do.

As a college teacher, I have written many letters of recommendation for students. I told each one of them that I would make an honest statement about the level of commitment they had made to their classwork. How would you fare out with such a recommendation?

To be trustworthy is gained only by your ability to make and finish commitments. It is a must attribute for you. Decide NOW!

Ready for the World

I dearly hope that you understand and fully accept the idea of the three magic words and will apply them to your life, now and for rest of your life.

> Independence
> Responsibility
> Commitment

In every situation that you meet, apply these three attributes with a passion. In doing so, it will take you to uncommon success. Therefore, it is time for you to tackle some important responsibilities. The balance of this book presents four great responsibilities that everyone faces. The material presented *will not* take you on a cookie cutter, step-by-step process because that simply won't work—one size does not fit all. Rather, the book will provide needed information and methods to solve the problems yourself. You, because you are independent, responsible, and committed, will make the best decisions for yourself.

Warning—The four areas listed below will require commitment and will take time, thoughtful deliberation, patience, and effort to accomplish. Stopping now because of that, would be a foolish thing to do. You see, with or without this book, you will face all four of these responsibilities whether you want to or not. Using this book with its guidelines, makes it possible for you to end up with great plans created by you, tailor made just for you.

These four areas of responsibility are:

Fiscal responsibility
Physical responsibility
Mental responsibility
Spiritual responsibility

You may take them in any order, depending on your greatest need. Continue to monitor your success with each plan as they are developed. By continued monitoring, you will discover better ways to function with that responsibility. Make the suggested changes and continue to monitor. The reality is that you are already living your life and dealing with the four responsibilities simultaneously, as we all must. You must have complete awareness of your activities always looking for a better way. It is not difficult for you to do this, you see, you are an independent, responsible, and committed person. Life will only get better.

God speed on your journey, Captain.

Websites on Being Responsible

Review the following websites to learn more about responsibility.

www.enotes.com/homework-help/why-responsibility-good-moral-value-281615
www.mdjunction.com/forums/agoraphobia-discussions/general-support/3254847-why-its-important-to-take-responsibility-for
www.vitalaffirmations.com/taking-responsibility.htm#.V7TGW5grKUk
www.positivityblog.com/index.php/2009/03/13/7-timeless-thoughts-on-taking-responsibility-for-your-life/
www.lifecoachexpert.co.uk/takingresponsibilityyouractions.html

CHAPTER TWO

Financial Responsibility

Becoming financially responsible means that you are in control of money rather than allowing money to be in control of you. It does not depend upon how much you earn, rather it depends upon what you do with what you earn. What a wonderful statement just for you. Here you are, an independent person not subject to the whims of advertisers, a person willing to take full responsibility to become financially responsible, and you are committed to make it happen. And it will.

What responsibilities do I face?

The first step means that you are fully responsible for providing for all of your own needs to function successfully in this world. If you marry and have children, you must also provide for all of them. Don't expect others to pay your way.

Yes, but it goes much further than that and will include many of the following situations.

Maintain life insurance
Maintain home insurance
Maintain health insurance
Maintain disability insurance
Maintain automobile insurance
Savings funds for the replacement of household equipment like oven, refrigerator, furniture, etc.
Educational funds for your children
Educational funds for you and your spouse's continuing education
Provide housing, food, and clothing
At least six months of salary available in case of a layoff or sick time
Funds for the annual family vacation
Funds for a down payment on a new home
Build short-term emergency funds
Build retirement funds

This is only a partial list, but it gives you the idea that there is much more than just paying the family bills. You *must* make arrangements to build short and long-term funds.

Ability to Save and Invest Dollars

At the start of each school semester, I would ask the students in my investment classes, "How many of you can save $25 a month"? Almost all the hands would go up. Next question, "How many of you save $25 each month?" Two or three hands would go up. The truth is that the vast majority of people can save money; they know they are supposed to, but they don't. The habit of spending every cent of earnings each month without regard to other needs is par for the course and continues for many years throughout their lives. Wow!

Saving is the only sure way to wealth!

The likelihood of saving is closely related to one's income. Thirty-nine percent of respondents with a household income under $40,000 per year saved some of their income in the past year, whereas 67% of those in the middle income group and 79% in the highest income group indicate that they saved a portion of their income. However, among those who saved at least a portion of their income, there are few differences in the average rate of savings, with those of all three income categories saving an average of 14 – 16% and a median of 10% of their income.

The survey asks those who saved to select all of the applicable reasons why they were saving. The top reasons for saving are for their retirement (57%), unexpected expenses (57%), and "just to save" (50%).

The frequency of these common reasons for savings differ based on where respondents fall in the income distribution. Among savers making over $100,000, retirement is the most commonly cited reason for saving—mentioned by 70% of respondents. This exceeds the 58% in this income group who are saving for unexpected expenses. The middle income category of respondents who saved some of their income say they are saving for retirement (54%) about as frequently as unexpected expenses (57%). However, among respondents who saved some of their income and make under $40,000, only 37% say that they are saving for retirement, compared to 53% who are saving for unexpected expenses.

(https://www.federalreserve.gov/econresdata/2014-report-economic-well-being-us-households-201505.pdf)

From the above data, it is clear that at least half of all families will retire with inadequate income. Please don't be one of them.

If the person earning $50,000 a year were to invest 5% of it throughout their working years, it would create a fund of $158,364. If this was to be their retirement income, it would be woefully inadequate. A person might also have a 401K and a Social Security check that would help but will still be inadequate for a good retirement. Truth is that many people may not have a 401K and may not qualify for social security, in which case, that person would be faced with frightfully inadequate income.

It is the author's contention that a person invest between 15% and 25% of their income each year up until retirement age. Why retire on a shoestring? The golden years are wonderful times and deserve financial freedom.

Beliefs that lead to financial failure:

> I will start investing when I earn more money.
> Buying "stuff" is more important that investing.
> Small savings won't amount to much.
> I can always meet my monthly payments.
> Learning to manage money is too hard.

We will go into more detail later but for a start let me help you get a better handle on what you are facing. From your monthly income, you will want to create three major investment funds.

You will want to do much more investing to do it properly. That, is the subject of this book.

Your savings funds are broken into three major groups:

> An emergency fund to handle unexpected health, automotive, or household expenses
> A fund to provide for living in case of a layoff from work
> A retirement fund, in addition to your Social Security and job retirement program

Obviously, if your savings must be split three ways, each account will have a meager beginning but they will grow. All accounts should be started at the same time, even if the amounts are small. The emergency fund is the more important one at the beginning. Why? If a sudden need arises and you don't have this fund, it will disrupt your overall budget. If you have the fund, it won't.

First create a fund to replace household items as they become unusable. Chances are that you are all set with these items and nothing needs replacement—good. This includes household repairs and large ticket items such as a refrigerator, washer, dryer, etc. The dollars will be there and not disrupt your regular budget. There is a chance that you have a debt from purchasing household items. If this is the case, continue paying off the debt then build the replacement fund. Think of how wonderful it would be if you could replace your refrigerator in the future with cash instead of debt.

The second most critical in the beginning is the fund in case of a layoff. How important this is will depend mainly on your type of work. If you are a construction worker, getting laid off in slow times is not unusual. You will want that fund to grow more quickly. Later, when you have six months of wages saved, you can move dollars into something else. Many have jobs that seem quite secure, but don't be deceived; there have been many surprise layoffs for a great variety of reasons. Be prepared for it and if it does not happen, you will have that much more for your retirement.

The third fund is for your retirement. This may be deceiving because you won't need it for a long time. It is a must to begin now because even small amounts invested over time will draw earnings and with compounding, will grow surprisingly well. Any time that you delay this, you must make up by doubling future investments.

You will determine how much to put into each fund when you get down to developing your budget later in this book.

What is Compounding

The magic of compounding is such that when you reach a certain dollar amount for some of your investment accounts, you can stop contributing. Why? Because the value of the account may be large enough that the earnings from the account will continue to make payments into it. In fact, when that happens, you can roll the continued earnings into the long-term investment for retirement to help it grow faster.

It is extremely important for you to understand compounding in order to appreciate the tremendous benefits of a long period of time. Compounding is the process of adding the annual earnings from an investment to the original investment, increasing the total investment value. That is, $1,000 invested at 8% will yield $80 in earnings in one year which is then added to the $1,000 for a new balance of 1,080. For the second year the interest of 8% based upon $1,080 is $86.40 and when added to the old balance, adds up to $1,166.40. Each year provides a larger amount of yield on the balance of the account. Let's examine Table 1 just below. What will the Investment look like in 10 years? The $1,000 investment earning 8% interest, will grow to $2,158.92. The interest earnings are more than the original investment of $1,000.

One Time Investment at 8% for 10 Years
Table 1

Year	Investment	Interest Earned	Balance
1	$1,000	$80.00	$1,080.00
2	$1,000	$86.40	$1,166.40
3	$1,000	$93.31	$1,259.77
4	$1,000	$100.78	$1,360.49
5	$1,000	$108.84	$1,469.33
6	$1,000	$117.55	$1,586.87
7	$1,000	$126.95	$1,713.82

8	$1,000	$137.11	$1,850.93
9	$1,000	$147.07	$1,999.00
10	$1,000	$159.92	$2,158.92
	Totals	$1,157.93	

If you were to leave this same investment until you retired at 65, it would be worth $17,245–quite amazing. It is important for you to notice the increase of the interest earned each year, that growth is the great importance of compounding.

Assuming you are in your twenties at the start, you have available to you the *single most important ingredient* for investing and that is TIME. The stark meaning of this is that you must start investing NOW; otherwise, you will eventually lose the great capacity to invest small dollars over a greater length of time.

What about some of you that may be in our 40's and 50's? If you have given away the time advantage and have very little invested, it is not too late. No, it's not too late, but you must overcome the problem of less time by investing larger amounts of principal. More on that later.

Table 1 shows a constant amount invested each month. In reality you will need to make monthly investments over a long period. It is amazing how much your investment will grow over time with small amounts like $50 or $100 each month. Table 2, *Periodic Payments over Time* will better help you understand compounding.

Periodic Payments Over Time
Table 2

Monthly Investment	Interest Rate	Ten Years	Twenty Years	Thirty Years	Forty Years
$50.00	8%	$9,208.28	$29,647.36	$75,014.70	$175,714.06
$100.00	8%	$18,416.57	$59,294.12	$150,029.52	$351,428.12
$200.00	8%	$36,833.14	$118,589.44	$300,059.04	$648,225.84
$300.00	8%	$55,249.70	$177,884.17	$450,088.55	$1,054,284.00

A 25 year old investing $50 each month can amass: $175,714.06 when reaching retirement years, 40 years. Your actual investment out of wages would be $24,000 per year, $50 a month for 40 years. That $24,000 would have earned $151,714.06 in dividend and interest payments for you during the 40-year period of investing. How to retire in style? Invest $200 a month on a regular basis and you can amass over one-half a million dollars. Can you see the power of compounding? If you do, you will waste no time in choosing to start your investment program. Read on and let's see how it can be done.

Dollar Averaging

There is an old saying that goes "it takes money to make money." Yes that is true but it doesn't mean someone with small amounts of cash cannot make money. Your only choice is to take a portion of your income and invest it regularly over a long period of time. This must be done faithfully, investing a portion of your income on a monthly basis. The goal will be to have the investment come out of your paycheck automatically. This is called *dollar averaging*.

A person selects a particular stock or mutual fund and contributes the same amount, on the same day each month. The money will buy a number of shares of that stock or mutual fund based upon the price of the stock that day. If a stock is **selling** for $10, $100 will buy 10 shares. The following month the stock price drops to $8 and your $100 will buy 12 ½ shares. Yes, some brokers will have programs to buy partial shares. The next month the stock goes to $12 and you will get 8 1/3 shares. You are now the proud owner of 30 5/6 shares. Soon, you will receive a notice that a dividend was paid to you, $.50 per share. That amounts to about $15.40. You wisely left instructions with your financial advisor to buy more stock with any dividends so the $15.40 buys a little more than one share. You now own 31 shares of stock, each selling for $12 putting your portfolio worth $372. You have invested $300 so you are $72 ahead.

The scary part occurs when you buy stock and its price drops and continues to stay low for an extended period. Do you bail out? To answer this question requires some bit of knowledge about what you bought and why you bought it. Let me illustrate with a story. Back in the mid 1950's, I decided to buy stock in the technical arena which tended to be a bit more risky but could also produce spectacular results if they hit it right. It was a very successful company that decided to go head-to-head with IBM in the computer mainframe industry. They invested considerable funds over three years without much success against Big Blue.

The stock price of the company started down from $20 per share to $15, then to $10 where it stayed a long time. Should I dump the stock and take a loss? I purchased the stock originally because this tech stock had a broad range of products like electric razors, typewriters, and useful household items that were selling very well. The profits remained strong and the quarterly dividends remained the same. The company paid a $.25 dividend each quarter which totaled a $1 each year. There is no way that I would sell for the return on my investment was 10% just in the dividends and the company was still very strong, regardless of poor computer manufacturing performance.

By the end of the third year I had amassed 360 shares purchased with additional shares from dividends to give me a total of 400 shares. One day the company announced success with its computer efforts and began giving IBM stiff competition. This good news meant much greater profits would be coming to the company. During the next year, the stock price shot up to $60 per share with an increase in dividends. At that point my stock portfolio was 400 shares at $60 each for a total value of $24,000. My investment was $100 a month for three years which was $3,600 invested. Most people would have bailed, but by sticking with the right information, it turned out to be one of my best investments ever.

What do you take away from this story? Stock prices are going to go up and then down. If you purchased a solid stock and price goes down—rejoice for your invested dollars will buy more shares. When the price goes back up a large number of shares at the increased price will make your portfolio look quite good. You can rejoice again. While the bottom line is that stock will go up and it will go down, if you bought quality stock it will go up more than it will go down as the company increases it sales and profits.

This is the system that you will use for investing. There is much more to it, but you need to have a good understanding of dollar averaging with its advantages and pitfalls.

Basic Investing Knowledge and Terminology

There are several misconceptions about investing that should be discarded. The first one is that because of the complexity of the investing world, you cannot participate successfully in it. Yes it is complex, but as we sift through the myriads of ideas, there is a basic foundation from which you can function. You need only to build this foundation and go to work. That is why we will continue presenting foundational information in this book. Of course you can function in it. Remember, as your portfolio grows your knowledge will also grow.

Another fallacy is that to earn the best money, you should trade stocks regularly always buying low and selling high. Please fully understand that you are not *trading stocks*; rather, *you are investing in stocks*. You are a long-term investor, not a stock trader. This means that you must select a stock that is priced right in the beginning, shows a great track record from the past, shows much promise for the future and is well managed. Gathering this information is not difficult nor is it too complex to understand. As long as your investment remains strong, you will keep on investing.

People think that the best buys are hot stocks that are soaring sky high with the general public in a frenzy to buy now. These stocks are generally to be avoided. Why? Because the high demand relative to the supply is causing the price to go unrealistically high. The company may be doing fine but the stock price is now much higher than the profit picture can support and the price cannot be sustained. Soon the wise investor will sell out. These are the traders. Wealthy sellers will sell large amounts of stock causing stock prices to spiral downward. In these cases, stocks often drop below what is their true value. You would be off to a very bad start buying at an extremely high price.

People also think that the investment field is difficult to understand, making good choices very risky. My investment classes were always concerned about this issue. The truth is that with some basic information you only need to be smart enough to walk to your bank and make an appointment with the investment advisor. He will be a skilled financial manager and will help you through the investing maze. He will listen to your story and come to understand all of your financial goals. Further, that person will help you with the broad base total financial planning in order to gain funds to invest. His company will be fully engaged in the analysis of many companies and can supply all of the information you need to make a wise choice. You can expect your financial manager to watch your various stocks and will notify you if something unusual is going on. Together you make a decision about what to do next.

Besides using your bank, there are other options available. There are many investment companies that are available. When the time comes to invest, visit several of them to see if they are interested in your business. Some companies specialize only in large investors and will require that you maintain a large account with them. Don't be discouraged about this. Do some homework before you begin looking for an advisor. Be aware that your credit union might be a great resource.

Whatever company you choose, develop a great relationship and get to know your advisor personally. The author has used the same company and advisor for 40 years and finds their services to be amazing. I receive monthly reports that show the status of every stock, when it was purchased, how much it has gained and current prices. All dividends are listed and show what additional stock was purchased from dividends. They provide a complete document for income tax purposes.

General Rules for Long-Term Investing

The investing world is very interesting but it is also very broad. During your lifetime, you will see many tempting offers usually touted to earn big dollars immediately. If such an offer sounds too good to be true, it likely will earn good profits but, usually only for the person selling the stock. All of your money could disappear instantly with rich sounding schemes. Stay on track throughout your investing life. The following list of rules is designed to pave the way for you. Obey them, and you will have success.

1. Buy stocks and mutual funds representing only the large, stable, and successful companies. My recommendation is to buy only stocks listed on the New York Stock Exchange.

The NYSE has stringent criteria for companies to meet before being accepted for trading. Remember, you are going for the long term. Many of us still own the same stocks that we bought many years ago and we rest with peace of mind. There are many corporations that have paid yearly dividends for many years. By law, these companies must maintain continual reports on their operations. This information is readily available.

2. Once you start dollar averaging, keep the perfect record of never missing an investment period.

When times get tough, there will be the temptation to use your investment dollars elsewhere. Don't do that. Missing once may not be a big deal, but can easily become a habit. If you never miss it once, you will continue as planned.

3. Direct a portion of every income raise to purchase additional stock by investing more into your current stock or start a new stock with the monthly increase. Further, dollars that you may get in larger sums should be invested into one of your successful holdings.

The author's rule was to direct one-half of all salary increases into the investment picture. When doing that, you will not miss the dollars going into the investment and can still appreciate the increase you get in your regular budget.

If you get the surprise of a large amount of money such as an inheritance, consider putting most or all of it into one of your successful investments. If you spend it all, whatever you bought will likely have depreciated to "0" in a few years and you will have no inheritance. If you invest it, you will likely earn twice as much as you originally received.

4. Never use your investment dollars to purchase *your current budget needs*.

There will always be the temptation to borrow from one of your funds to pay for short-term needs. Avoid this at all cost and find another way to deal with the problem.

5. Diversify your stock holdings.

There is an old axiom that says *don't put all of your eggs in one basket*. This is true of investments. In the beginning you will likely buy one stock or one mutual fund. As you have increased funds to invest it is best to pick a second company that provides a different product than the first investment. You immediately create diversity and this same process should be followed each time you increase your dollars into investments.

This will be especially true if you start with stock of one company. One manufacturing company might produce paint, for example. This company will likely have different colors and different kinds of paint, but it is still paint. If the construction business slows down in the USA, paint production would likely fall off. It might be wise for you to consider your first investment in mutual funds. A mutual fund is a company that takes dollar investments from people and purchases a variety of different common stocks with the money. The result is that you will have immediate ownership of one mutual fund company stock but that represents a portion of ownership in all of varied holdings of the mutual fund. You get immediate diversification.

What determines whether you start by purchasing stock in a mutual fund as opposed to stock in a corporation such as IBM, Kroger Food Store, or Alcoa, manufacturers of aluminum products?

The financial advisor that you choose will likely be able to help you with that question. It will depend much upon the skill and understanding that you bring into the process. To buy one stock will take more expertise in completing the necessary analysis to make the purchase decision. Keep reading and studying and you will find the answer.

P/E Ratio and Yield

We begin by giving you the most basic, important information. That information is based upon how much a stock earns but always in relationship to its selling price and how much of the earnings is given to the stockholders.

P/E ratio compares the price of a stock with earnings. If stock A sells for $65 with earnings of $5 per share and stock B sells for $148 earnings of $8 per share, which stock has the greater earning power? This is determined by using the Price to Earnings ratio, that is, divide the earnings into the price. $65 divided by $5 provides a ratio of 13:1. That translates to the notion that it takes $13 to get a $1 return for stock A. For stock B, we divide the price $148 by $8 which provides a ratio of 16:1. That means it requires $16 to earn a $1 return for stock B, the better investment appears to be stock A, at 13 to 1 ratio. Stock A has better earning power.

Here is a listing of several stocks. Use the P/E ratio to determine the one with the most earning power.

Stock	Price	Earning	P/E Ratio
Stock A	$320	$18.00	
Stock B	$ 14	$ .70	
Stock C	$ 88	$ 3.00	
Stock D	$179	$ 9.00	

Answers:

Stock A	17.70
Stock B	20.00
Stock C	29.30
Stock D	19.90

Stock A appears best because $17.70 will earn $1 of profit. Stock C is the poorest as it requires $29.30 of investment to reap $1 of profit. The P/E ratio provides only a starting point as there are other issues to study. Now that you understand it, we'll use it later as you learn more.

To summarize, we can say that a stock with a very low ratio such as 10:1 has good earning power and a stock with a 50:1 ratio is not producing much in earnings compared to the stock price. Please remember that these numbers are only a starting point. There are cases where a low P/E may look good but is dangerous without further investigation. The following example represents a company which has had good power in the past but did not keep up with technology changes in its products. Their current P/E ratio is 9:1, but the company is headed for a big fall. Smart investors will spot this and begin selling, causing the price to go down rapidly, which results a low P/E ratio. Soon after, profits will begin dropping rapidly. You would be purchasing a loser.

Yield is a brother to the P/E ratio. X company may have $7 of earnings but the earnings remain in the company and are invested in some business activity. The money would be used internally by the company and stockholders would get $0 of the $7 earnings. The Board of Directors would look at the $7 of earnings and the company cash needs to determine a possible dividend for the stockholders.

The Board might decide to declare a dividend of $4 leaving $3 in the company to help it grow. If the value of X Company stock is $75 the P/E ratio would be 10:1—good earning power. The yield of a stock is the dividend paid on each share of stock relative to the cost of the stock. This is done by dividing the dividend by the stock price—that is $4 divided by $75, the price. This yields a 5.4% profit per share to each shareholder.

To summarize, the earnings (profit) of the company is usually split between funding needed for business activities and profit returned to the shareholders who expect some return for their investment. The portion of earnings kept by the corporation to fund growth is called retained earnings. The portion of the earnings given to the shareholders is called dividends.

Income vs Growth Stock

Should you buy a stock that pays a high yield or a low yield? That will depend mainly upon your personal investment goal. A young investor is going for the long haul and wants growth. Another investor is older and ready to begin withdrawing funds for retirement. The older person should buy an income stock and the younger person a growth stock.

An income stock is one that has good earning power and pays out almost all earnings per share to the stockholders. The stockholder can withdraw the cash for living purposes. But if the company pays out most of its earnings, the retained earnings do not grow, the company grows only minimally and stock prices increase only minimally. The yield to the shareholder may be as high as 8% or more. This would be a good investment because of the high dividend rate, but the stock most likely will see very little upward price change. The company will be unable to grow because it retains no fund to help it do so. This is good for a retired investor—they are not concerned with price increase but more concerned with highest rate of current dollar return.

The growth stock is a perfect fit for the long-term investor. Lower dividend mean higher retained earnings which will fuel growth. Growth means increased production, increased sales, and increased profits. The profits are what fuel stock price increases. Look for companies that have a low P/E ratio with a low yield to get the greatest long-term gain. The thing to fully understand here is the difference between an income and a growth stock. Your investment advisor will help you decide which stock is an investment stock vs. a growth stock.

Reviewing Your Budget to Start Investing

Please fully digest the first few pages of this chapter and put them firmly in your mind. These are the basis for investing but there is more to come. For now we are going to review your personal spending habits and to rearrange spending habits to find dollars to invest. This is not painful; rather, it is ultimately a refreshing process. Why is this? It will change your life for the better. How will it do so? Most everyone in the USA practices foolish spending, foolish in that you really didn't need the items and they were painfully expensive. Most important, people spend much of their money buying negative things that tend to destroy good health.

The first of these is drinking too much alcohol. Nothing wrong with beer, but a six pack all at once! You are not only getting fat, that's expensive. Colas and other soda products are expensive and laced with sugar and quite unhealthy. If you don't believe that, just notice the huge increase in diabetes. Find healthy drinks and drink only as needed. Why not just drink more water. Another big negative is smoking. I could never understand why some people are willing to pay so much to gain poor health. Just the dollars spent alone on smoking would generate a tidy sum to invest.

After that comes a whole army of crummy spending habits, such as eating out too often, buying impulse items in the store (things you really didn't need), money wasted in slot machines, buying designer clothes that you really don't need—and the list goes on.

Honest Budgeting

Working with people through the years to create a budget has been most interesting. Most everyone has all kinds of justifications for engaging in poor spending habits, but once we talk through the issues and they choose to be honest, making changes was very productive and resulted in positive cash flow available for investing.

Once a person affects the changes in spending and begins the process of budgeting and investing, they tend to feel good about what they have done and most go on to unusual success. What they have done is to exercise their independence, clarify and fully accept their responsibilities, and finally made the commitment necessary for success. I have yet to meet an investor who was dissatisfied with having to create a usable budget.

Enter your net salaries (after taxes) from all sources in the cash flow worksheet that follows. Blank lines are available from possible other sources such as unemployment checks, alimony or child support, family or friends, etc. Some dollars that you receive may come in a lump sum. Enter the lump sum into the Annual Income column then divide by 12 to get the monthly income and enter it in the Monthly Income column. Do not include income that is not available for spending such as interest on investments or stock dividends. Those dollars go back into the investment.

If good things happen during the year such as a pay raise, update the cash flow worksheet immediately.

Cash Flow Worksheet

Income Source	Monthly Income	Annual Income
Husband Salary		
Wife Salary		
Part-time Work		
Rental Income		
Income Tax Return		
Bonuses		
Gifts		
Dollars from Investments		
Other		
Total		

Hopefully, you have included all possible and likely income into the cash flow worksheet. You now know exactly the monthly cash flow dollars.

Expenses

Certain expenses are variable each month such as utilities. Calculate the annual cost for these and divide by 12 to find the average monthly cost. For periodic expenses such as insurance and vehicle registration, estimate the yearly cost then divide by 12 to calculate the monthly.

Expense Item	Monthly Expenses	Annual Expenses
Home Expenses		
Home Insurance		
HOA/Condo Fees		

Mortgage/Rent		
Maintenance		
Gas		
Electric		
Water/Sewer		
Yard Care		
Other		
Food:		
Groceries/Household Items		
Work/School Lunch		
Other		
Insurance:		
Health		
Vision		
Dental		
Disability		
Medical Care:		
Doctor		
Chiropractor		
Eye		
Dental		
Orthodontist		
Medication		
Medical Supplies		
Dental		
Medication		

Transportation:		
Car Payment 1		
Car Payment 2		
Auto Insurance		
Registration/License		
Gasoline		
Oil Changes		
Repairs		
Parking		
Tolls		
Child Care:		
Alimony		
Child Support		
Day Care Diapers/Baby Supplies		
Baby Equipment		
Loan Payments		
Credit Card 1		
Credit Card 2		
Credit Card 3		
Personal:		
Beauty/Barber		
Clothing		
Jewelry		
Cosmetics		
Manicure		

Enertainment:		
Cable/Satellite		
CD's.Tapes/ DVD's		
Sports		
Hobbies		
Movies		
Dining Out		
Vacation/Travel		
Miscellaneous		
Bank Fees		
Laundry		
Union/Other Dues		
Internet Service		
Pet Care		
Birthday Gifts		
Cell Phone/Pager		
Postage		
Alcohol		
Cigarettes		
Church/Charity		
Taxes:		
Federal Tax with Return		
State Tax with Return		
Estimated Quarterly Tax		
Other:		

Totals		

Expenses Balance

You should now have the Income and Expense worksheets filled in. You will want to go through your checkbook stubs and review the various expense items. If you find something not listed on the income or expense worksheets, make the entry now. This process works only as you have included all possible expense and income items.

It's time to take stock and make some decisions. Total the monthly columns for both Income and Expenses. Subtract the total per month Expense from the total per month Income. Hopefully there is a strong positive balance. These are the dollars that you may assign into the various investment and bank accounts.

If there is a small positive balance or a negative balance, it means decision time regarding both your Income and your Expenses. In order to gain a larger positive balance, you must begin by going through each Expense item and evaluate the possibility of reducing as many as you can. Incidentally, you should do this examination even if you came out with a strong positive balance. You may discover some foolish spending that could be recovered. It will increase your positive balance for investing. This whole goal is to discover a better way to use your dollars. From it you will end up living a healthier life.

Following are some ideas that you may apply in the evaluation process. Please be very honest in your choices always put being responsible at the head of every decision.

1. Some items that appear to be fixed monthly expenses could be altered to improve cash flow.
    a. Look into remortgaging your home with a lower interest rate thus reducing the monthly payment.
    b. Do you have an automobile that is expensive? Think about making a swap to get a less expensive dependable automobile. It can reduce your car payments, insurance, license, and fuel costs.
    c. Look for a better bargain on your current insurance policies. Be sure to include:
        i.   Automobile
        ii. Home owners

       iii. Health

       iv. Disability

       v. Other

   d. Look for a way to consolidate your current debt to reduce total payments.

2. Try changing your thermostat to reduce electricity and fuel costs. A change is sometimes for the better for you.

3. Consolidate your trips and drive less miles.

4. If you have not done so, begin using coupons for various purchases. You would be amazed at how much can be saved.

5. Change your eating-out habits and cook more at home. It's much cheaper.
   a. Find less expensive restaurants that serve good food.
   b. Cut way down on the *big gulp* drinks. You'll save a bundle and improve your health—way too much sugar and other bad stuff!
   c. Stop going to fast food restaurants.
   d. Find coupons for the restaurants you favor.
   e. Car pool.

6. Stop your purchase of impulse items. These items are strategically placed at the end of aisles where the customer almost bumps into them. Between the kids begging you to buy or somehow thinking you might need it, you money is gone. But it makes a nice garage sale item. STOP foolish spending.

7. Consider cutting back on your personal care items. Just do what you really need, not what you want.

8. Try to repackage your Internet, cable, and telephone to reduce some of the costs by choosing only the services you really need.

9. A glass of wine is delightful. Trouble is—the American way is *more is better*. Not true. If you are in a position to both save money and improve your health—do so.

10. Cigarette smokers think about giving up smoking. Trade the cost of cigarettes for some great investments, you'll end up rich and can enjoy yourself without COPD. Look the enemy straight in the eye and say *down with you*, and mean it. Lots of folks have done just that quite successfully.

11. Go all through every expense item and apply your most creative ideas—who knows how you can improve things.

If you found a number of changes that you want to make, make them now on the worksheet before continuing to your finished product. You can't really finish until you know exactly what you have. Remember also to review your income items to determine if they can be improved and enter the figure in the income section. Subtract your monthly and annual expenses from your monthly and annual income.

Hopefully you have been able to improve your positive balance of available dollars. We now want to look at this positive balance and decide how much should go into each of 5 investments accounts.

These accounts are:
Home emergency fund
Lay-off fund
Household equipment replacement fund and home maintenance
Retirement investment fund
Children's college fund
Bank account

These accounts will vary considerably between families as there are so many different possibilities in people's situations. To help you divvy up the dollars, I have created a fictitious family that might represent the mainstream young person as an example.

Will Schaffer is 25 years old and his wife Janice is 24. They met in high school, married young and currently have two children 2 and 4. He worked in a print shop while in high school and came to appreciate the higher levels of skill in his profession. He learned the craft well and is currently employed by the same company. A nice salary came with the skill level. His take-home salary is $3,250 each month, net. His wife, Janice, has acquired a part-time job with a local flower shop and also contributes $1,595 each month. Her mother helps look after the children while Janice is at work.

Will participates in a 401K retirement program through his company which contributes only minimally toward their retirement. One of their friends is a banker and has helped them with their budgeting so they do much better than most people their age. The banker recommends that Will and Janice start investment programs aiming to invest 10% to 15% of their net monthly income. Their target for total monthly investments would be approximately 12% of their monthly net income. That would result in investing $500 every month.

Fortunately, Will read this book and is looking to satisfy the various saving needs. Besides the four funds discussed in this book, Will and Janice know that they must start a college fund for their children, but they felt that the emergency fund was the current highest priority. Their reasoning was that without this fund to cover immediate financial problems (such as car repairs), it would be a serious interruption to their financial planning. They decided that the emergency fund ultimate balance should be $3,500 and they would maintain that balance for three years. They chose to put $80 monthly into the emergency fund. Whenever the fund reached the goal, the monthly payment would be diverted to one of the other investments.

Will and Janice considered the second priority to be the household replacement fund. Their reasoning was, if we start now, in 8 years when a major appliance might go bad, the dollars will be in the fund. They love the idea of paying cash and avoiding the need to borrow money thus avoiding paying extra interest cost. They agreed on $80 to be invested monthly until a balance of $900 is reached. That will take some time, but their current appliances should last that long.

The next fund of importance is the college fund. In 14 years, their oldest child will start college and for several years, they will have both children in college. They allot $70 a month to the children's college fund. The plan is to divert the invested dollars from the emergency to the college fund when the emergency fund balance is met.

The layoff fund is not critical for Will. Printing is a very stable industry and Will has been promised a continued upgrading of his skills increasing his salary. However low the probability of lay-off, there is always a possibility. They choose to invest $40 each month into the lay-off fund.

Will and Janice, realizing the great benefit from compounding decide to contribute as much as possible into their retirement investments. They chose to start investing $200 a month. Their banker friend helped them make the investment choice.

Their plan is to increase the contributions to their investment program as they receive increased salaries. For each raise, they will evaluate where the increased amounts should be invested.

Summary of the Action

Emergency fund $80 per month   Goal $3,500
   With interest earned on the investment, it will reach the $3,500 balance in approximately three years.

Household Replacement $80 per month   Goal $1,800
   With interest earned on the investment it will reach the $1,800 balance in approximately two years.

College Fund $70 per month   Goal Variable

With interest earned on the investment for a minimum of 12 years, the fund should total approximately $17,000 when the first child is ready for college.

| Lay-off Fund | $40 per month | $6,000 |

With interest earned on the investment for 10 years, the fund should show a total of approximately $7,300.

| Retirement Fund | $200 per month | Goal Retirement Age |

With interest earned on the investment for 40 years, the fund should show a total of approximately $703,000.

Will and Janice plan to manage certain changes as they go along with the plan. These will include:

As funds reach their goals, move the monthly investments to the fund in most need at that time.

The retirement fund investment will be increased out of wage increases. Their goal is to reach at least $1,000,000 at retirement.

At retirement time, they will move any unneeded balance in the other funds to the retirement fund. Assuming that the investment plan earns 8% or more, they plan to draw only 5% of the total from the fund for retirement. Five percent of $1,000,000 would provide $50,000 each year to go along with their 401K and Social Security. What a nice retirement they are facing.

If the investment fund at the time of retirement is earning 8% and if they withdraw only 5%, the $1,000,000 will continue to grow. Their plan is that it will provide a great contingency against disaster and they plan on helping their grandchildren with college. They also like the idea of leaving a legacy to their children. They will not spend the $1,000,000 just because they have it.

The Bank Account

You may have noticed that they have invested $470 each month from the $500 available. The difference should remain in the bank account to grow. At the rate of $30 each month, their bank account will increase $360 annually. Not a whole lot, but over time it will build. Consider this an additional safety net if something goes wrong. Don't spend it just because it is available.

There are several issues that remain. The first is that the monthly investment of $470 will be split into purchasing three different mutual funds. They do not need to be in separate accounts;

rather, all of the stock will be in one fund. The bookkeeping is done using the information in the account summary table below:

Investment Account Summary

Account Title	Monthly Investment	$ Goal
Emergency Fund	$80	$3,400
Household Replacement	$80	$1,800
College Fund	$70	$17,000
Lay-off Fund	S40	$6,000
Retirement Fund	$200	Unlimited
Bank Account	$30	Unlimited

Since the total dollars are all in one investment account, Will and Janice will use the above table to determine the approximate value of each account as needed. If after two years, it is necessary to use any account, merely multiply the monthly investment amount by the number of months invested. That will tell you approximately how much is available to use. For example, in December of the second year, they need money to pay for a surprise expense, they would multiply the age of the account (months) by the monthly investment. That would be 24 times $80 and come to a total of $1,920 available.

Special Note: Will and Janice were already doing a good job with their finances and there was plenty of excess to invest. You may find that the dollars available to you are skimpy. Don't give up, split up the funds as described, even if it is only $10 a month for some of the funds. Take the total and invest it in one mutual fund to start, keeping your investment account summary. Later, as your income increases and as you discover new ways to save on your spending, you can increase the investment accounts. The most important thing that you can do now is to START!

If you don't start, you won't get there.

Accounting for the Various Investment Funds

All of your dollars will go into the one investment fund, but you must know how much is growing in each account. Do this by studying the table above and estimate a date when you will have met the maximum requirements. As you invest, the dollars will build up in each account until your goal for each is met. Continue making your regular investments but the amount over and above the goals will be credited to your retirement account which will now grow faster.

Making Your First Investment

Alright, you have readjusted your budget and found some dollars to invest. Now what? Go talk with the investment advisor at your bank or credit union or both. Let them know that you want to invest X amount of dollars each month in the same stock or mutual fund for an extended period. Listen to their thoughts on your idea and discuss what they can do for you. He/she will want to know about you, your job, goals, income, etc.

The advisor will put your ideas together and suggest a plan. Try to keep it so that you buy the selected stock each month, and you should expect a small normal brokerage fee for that service.

Listen to what they have to say, and determine if you feel confident in their ideas. Assess the variety of options they may have and make a choice. If you are not comfortable thank them for visiting with you and talk to another bank.

Other options include using a company that specializes in helping people make investments. Call and talk with one of them about what you plan to do. Some companies will only accept clients that make large investments, but many are willing to work with the small investor. Don't be discouraged if one is not interested, just call another.

Edward Jones Investments has offices all over the country and there is likely an office close to you. Start with them. The author uses Morgan Stanley and finds them to be really good. Give your local Morgan Stanley a call. There are other good ones, just look for them by searching for investment companies on the web.

There are a number of good investment companies that you will find on the Internet. Try Vanguard.com and Fidelity.com. If you like talking online, there is a wealth of services offered by these companies. You will also have access to advisors over the telephone. Try it, you might like it.

Life Insurance

There are many options for the purchase of life insurance. You will need to sift through the various offerings and make a choice. I have included a basic theory for consideration.

At the beginning of your adult life having the insurance safety net is extremely important. We read of incidents of a young person dying from an accident. This is usually followed by car washes and other donation schemes in order to pay for last costs, let alone the loss of income from the deceased. A young person can buy term life insurance at a very nominal rate that would ease the problem. If you are young and married with children, life insurance is a must.

My personal theory has worked something like this. At age 20, I had some investment, but only minimal and it would not pay for the last costs in case of my demise. I married while in college but still continued to invest in my retirement accounts. Soon two children came along and the need for life insurance became paramount. In my first job, my wife was a stay at home mom and provided no income which meant that my family would be in deep trouble in case of my demise.

Having only minimal investments, my only recourse was to buy term life insurance. It was quite inexpensive and I could buy enough to ensure a reasonable life style for my family if I died. For most people, at this time in their life, their investment pot would be close to zero and their insurance needs quite high. A graph of the needs for a young person with family might look something like this:

Figure 1

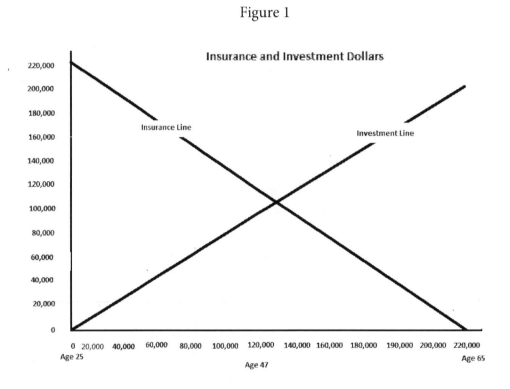

At age 25 with a family, a person would need considerable insurance. Study the graph lines and note that at age 25 the owner buys $220,000 worth of insurance. If that person has no investments, there is zero financial protection for his family. Notice that the investment line starts at zero on the chart but grows over time.

As the investment increases, there is less need for the large amounts of insurance so that the family can begin reducing the amount of insurance needed, thus allowing them to put the saved dollars into the investment side. As a person gets to 47 years of age, the investment may be worth $120,000 so the family may wish to drop the insurance to $80,000 to still provide a total of $120,000 in the estate, the amount they would have if the breadwinner passed away. Actually, as the value of the investment grows, it can be accompanied by a corresponding decrease in the need for insurance. Just simply buy less insurance when you start a new term.

As the estate reaches the financial target, there would be enough funds to support the cost of a funeral, and with adequate health insurance you could completely drop the cost of life insurance.

The Nature of Life Insurance

The cost of basic insurance is a pure, raw expense, to cover a possible disaster. You must study the insurance picture and be sure to understand the various kinds of policies available.

Let's look at the most basic life insurance—it's called term insurance because it is purchased in five year blocks with the cost of a block quite inexpensive at a younger age. The reason for the low cost is that a young person at age 25 is not at high risk to die. Five years later, at age 30, the premium on the policy will go up in cost. That will happen every five years of your life. The problem arises when you are 70 years old as the policy cost will be very expensive because you are at a much higher risk of dying. If you stop paying the premium the policy ends and all that you paid during the preceding years would be pure raw expense. Term insurance may also be sold in 10 year terms as well as 5 year terms.

There are several kinds of life insurance policies where you will pay an increased amount of premium which not only buys your basic life insurance but will build cash value over your life. By adding extra dollars to the premium, a cash value will build so that in time the policy might be paid in full. One of those options is ordinary insurance where the premium is lower and cash value builds slowly and you will pay the premium for most of your life. The advantage is that you are paying a constant premium over your life. There are other policies called limited-pay policies. The premium cost will be higher but the cash build up is greater and the policy will be paid for after 20 or 30 years. The cash build up belongs to the insured and can be cashed in at any time. You have the option to take the cash build up but the insurance will stop. You can leave the balance with the insurance and the amount of insurance on the policy will remain in force.

In my own case, I bought two policies called whole life insurance. After a few years, I realized the small amount of return on the cash value of my policy was not acceptable. I cashed in both policies and received $6,000 with which I bought a term policy with a higher value than the insured value of the two policies and invested the rest—dollar averaging. This was a wise move as the $6,000 investment did very well over the next years.

Once you hit the peak of your investment goals, stop the purchase of term life insurance and invest in more stock and invest the savings into more stock. I stopped buying any life insurance a number of years ago, because at that time there was enough value in the investment fund to easily pay for any last costs plus generate retirement income for many years for my heirs.

The amount of insurance you buy will vary because of the various income levels, various ages, various goals, and various responsibilities. The Internet will be of great help on this one.

In your financial planning, consider all of the issues that must satisfy both you and your family. Will you be receiving any inheritance? Does your spouse have a profession and a salary that will sustain the family? When will the home mortgage be paid off? When will the children leave the nest? What is your debt level? Make your planning program complete.

Buying Your Home

Your home is not only your family haven; it is also a great investment. Once purchased, home values will generally increase in value over time. The loan used to purchase the home will gradually be paid off, increasing the equity in the investment. At some point in the future you will end up with a fully paid for valuable asset.

In order to protect yourself and make this work as it should, there are some rules you must follow for complete success. Unfortunately, people will attach other desires to home buying, usually paying a heavy price. First are the rules for success.

1. Try to make a substantial down payment on your new home. It will reduce the monthly mortgage payments and will start you with a fair equity in the home.

2. Shop for your mortgage. Home lending is a competitive business and one can find the best deal shopping round. Look for the lowest interest rate, although the industry stays pretty close on this. Be sure to get the best payment terms that fit you. Be fully aware of possible hidden costs and understand that you will likely borrow at a discount. As an example, you might pay $202,000 for borrowing $200,000. The $2,000 is a discount fee going to the lender, and you will sign a $202,000 mortgage when you only needed $200,000. This procedure is common, but lenders will vary on the amount sometimes with no discount at all.

3. My recommendation is that you secure a 15 year mortgage as opposed to a 30 year mortgage. The monthly payments will be higher but bite the bullet and do it. While the 30 year mortgage is easier on your bank account, in the short run you will pay an enormous amount of interest for the extra 15 years, probably doubling the interest costs over the life of a 15 year mortgage. One of my daughters and her husband took a 15 year mortgage on their home, and now in their 40's, will have the home paid for in three years. Imagine, their normal monthly house payment of $1,600 will now be invested regularly into their retirement investment account. That in itself will generate

a very tidy sum over the next 15 years. The interest rate is usually less on a 15 year mortgage. Over the lifetime of the mortgage, you will save a bundle of interest dollars.

A large number of people make some basically serious errors regarding their home investment. Following, are some of the pitfalls.

1. Refinancing to get ready cash. A nice equity build up can be a strong temptation. Hey, my house is now worth $300,000 and the mortgage is down to $190,000. I'll get a second mortgage and use the cash; after all, I *want* it. Big time error! To use long-term borrowed money to finance short term needs is idiotic. Whatever you buy will be gone in several years or sooner yet you will continue paying for another 15 to 30 years. I have a friend who used a second mortgage to buy a motorcycle. The motorcycle is long gone but he'll be paying for it for another 25 years. Then, by a stroke of bad luck, the economy went south, the value of his house went south and now he is upside down. That is where the value of the home is below the mortgage value. With interest cost, he'll end paying over $100,000 dollars for the motorcycle.

2. Refrain from putting a second mortgage on your home. The interest cost for a second mortgage will be higher, perhaps significantly higher. This is so because the second mortgagor is in a second position to the first and is less likely to get repaid if there is a default. The problem is that securing a second is relatively easy to do. If you stay true to your goal to get equity built as fast as possible, there will be no need for a second.

3. Take great care in reorganizing your financial affairs where your home is concerned. There might come a time when a hardship comes your way and changes must be made. Do not, if at all possible, use your home as this buffer. The only avenue where the home might be concerned is to consider remortgaging your home. If current mortgage rates have gone down significantly, you might consider securing a new mortgage at the lower rate in hopes that it will reduce your monthly mortgage costs. However, do not give away any equity. If you have equity built in your home, there will be a temptation to increase the mortgage amount to gain immediate cash. That is a no-no. And if you do remortgage, try to keep the remaining life of the mortgage to a low figure. Be satisfied with a monthly payment decrease.

4. If you sell your home you may receive a nice cash settlement. Do not spend one penny on "stuff;" rather, invest all of it in your new home and reduce the mortgage keeping the house payments low.

Be like the bull dog that protects his bone. Do the same with your home. Good luck!

The Final Word

Remember that your goal is to provide for you and your family as long as you live. In other words, be financially responsible for as long as you live. There will be temptations along the way as your wealth increases which could include, I want that new car so bad, my friend told me of an investment that will earn a bundle quickly, or my son has a financial problem so let's use some of our investment to help. If you want to do those things, do it without touching your long-term investments.

God Speed on your journey, Captain.

Epilogue

I want to offer some thoughts on the purpose of building wealth. This book serves the purpose of getting you started to take advantage of a long period of time in which your savings can grow and build so that your family will have what they need now and later in life. Getting rich so that your life is filled with having lots of toys and an upscale life style would be a serious error

You must remain focused on a much higher set of values. Your family, your friends, your personal growth, serving others as you can, staying healthy, your personal faith journey, your gifts to charity and so on are the mainstream of your life. Use your wealth to assure health for yourself and your family.

At the start of each semester I would ask students in the investment classes, "would having $5,000,000 solve most of your problems?" Almost all would answer "yes" to that question. In reality, it would cause many people to change their lives to a big show and tell game likely doing more harm than good. There are any number of people where winning the lottery destroyed them.

One's wealth must be used wisely!

Special Thoughts on Dying

Seem like a morbid subject? Really not, as we all will face it one day. Death is really quite a natural thing but I think like most things, it is ignored until that time comes. People should determine well before hand how the event of dying should be handled. Act now so it will ease the burden at that time of demise.

When my wife and I were in our 50's we sat down to talk about dying to find out what we each might want. It happened that we both preferred cremation so we began searching for how to get that service. In our search we came across a company named the Neptune Society whose services included taking care of everything related to the dying including: Picking up the body wherever it is whether it be a foreign country or anyplace in the USA. They would arrive to pick up the body within an hour and will take care of all legal issues and secure a death certificate. The price included giving us the beautiful containers that will hold the ashes. No need to call the paramedics or the hospital, just one phone call.

Their services convinced us to join the society so we both carry a card instructing anyone on what to do when dying occurs. With that financial part taken care of the next subject is that of the funeral expenses.

We have bypassed the process of buying a casket and the funeral services a mortuary would provide. There is also the cost of paying for a burial plot. That problem would be eliminated if you chose to spread the ashes over a lake, river or park, a place that the deceased loved. In our case we much prefer to use our church where a memorial service would be held.

My wife and I have chosen to be buried in a military cemetery where the military will conduct a lovely service. Our demise will be cost free and easy to deal with. Our cost in dying fully paid for.

Websites on Financial Success

Review the following websites to learn more about investing.

https://www.balancetrack.org/home/10steps/index.html
http://www.moneycrashers.com/achieve-financial-success/
http://www.wikihow.com/Invest-Small-Amounts-of-Money-Wisely
http://money.usnews.com/money/blogs/the-smarter-mutual-fund-investor/2012/10/03/new-to-investing-use-dollar-cost-averaging
http://www.cfinancialfreedom.com/11-tips-invest-money-wisely/
http://www.thesimpledollar.com/six-steps-for-a-beginning-stock-investor/
http://www.investopedia.com/articles/retirement/06/10secureretirementtips.asp
http://www.investopedia.com/university/stocks/stocks1.asp
http://einvestingforbeginners.com/2013/04/10/how-to-calculate-pe-ratio/
http://www.businessinsider.com/amazing-power-of-compound-interest-2014-7

CHAPTER THREE

Physical Health—Eating Right

Welcome to that which is more important to your life than anything else. Why is this statement so true? Because without good health, you cannot function properly and would be unable to accomplish the other responsibilities you face. But the deceiving parts of poor health habits are not often noticed in the early part of life.

One can eat poorly and refrain from exercise for a while and it will seem to make no difference. Unfortunately, people become addicted to this life style. At midlife, when one is overweight and not feeling well, difficulties begin to arise.

The author is currently advising an overweight woman who is working as a registered nurse. Because of being on her feet for twelve-hour shifts, her knees are failing and she has only two choices--big time surgery or retirement. What awful choices at age 50. She also faces a third choice, to begin eating healthy and regain the strength to do her work and *live her life comfortably*. The most difficult choice for her now is changing to a healthy lifestyle. This one is a must, or the rest of her life will be in turmoil. I hope that you get the point. *Lousy eating habits and no exercise lead to big problems.*

We are talking about a life-style change that will reap many rewards. Think of what it would mean to have perfect health. You would always feel good with plenty of energy to accomplish your goals. A strong body will ward off many illnesses. You will greatly improve the possibility of avoiding major catastrophes such as heart problems, cancer, diabetes, etc.

Our physical health is made up of both the diet and the exercise. The term diet refers to the selection of food that you choose to eat. People will argue whether diet is more important than exercise, but in the final analysis, they are both important and must be in sync to work really well. We will begin discussion on the diet side.

A New Approach to Diet

The purpose for eating food is to nourish the body and make you healthy and feel good. Many people are prone to eat for emotional reasons such as escaping from boredom, nervousness, getting hooked on a special taste, or myriad of other reasons. You must always keep it clear in your mind, *eat for the purpose of being healthy and fit*. Anything else might be a negative.

A Perspective

Unfortunately, most people take the word diet to be very difficult and think they have to give up something they love. Let's reverse this idea to gain a broad and healthy perspective to see eating properly as a marvelous healing process.

First, there are thousands of different food products to choose from. Rather than see it as giving up something you want, see it as a myriad of possible choices to provide good health. Most of us have perhaps 20 or 30 food choices within our usual diet. Some of these will include food items that you definitely don't want to give up, perhaps onion rings or French fries may be one of these. In the case where you must stop eating your favorite food, see it as searching the vast array of food products to replace it with something healthier and just as tasty. If you choose right, the craving for the one you gave up will disappear.

Why is this so important? The food industry is part of our great free economic system and much of what it produces is good and healthy. This means that they are also free to create foods that are tastier and will have longer shelf life. Unfortunately, this leads to food additives such as salt, sugar or chemical additives that provide a longer shelf life. While this may increase sales for business, it can lead to long-term health problems for consumers. There is also the problem of food growers adding chemicals to grow products faster and bigger. Unfortunately, these chemicals build toxins which also lead to health problems. It is essential that you take full control of the eating process to remain physically fit. Most of us do not have enough information to make good choices. This chapter is mostly a course in creating a perfect diet.

Summary: See proper diet as making the best choices from the vast array of foods available for consumption. Finding a new and healthy eating regimen is exciting and highly rewarding.

Special Note: Of course--we should be ready and willing to give up certain foods as they may be a serious detriment to good health. Do not mourn the loss; rather rejoice in the freedom that you have to make another choice. That's a healthy perspective!

Personal Diet

All of you are eating according to a diet that you have chosen. If you haven't given much thought about what goes into your body, you will need to change that. Often, when our personal diet is not working, we look for one of the many planned diets such as:

Gluten Free
DASH (Dietary Approaches to Stop Hypertension, highly regarded for general use)
Atkins
Jenny Craig
Weight Watchers

Choosing one of these may work for a while, but we tend to swing back into the old habits. Why? One size does not fit all and the other problem is far more important. You still have very little understanding about what goes into your body. If you don't fully understand what you are doing to your body, you cannot make a commitment to it. Our approach to your diet is that you come to understand what your body needs and provide it by making intelligent, specific choices. This certainly will require more work but the payoff is bigtime.

Kidney Failure

The author has a friend whose kidneys failed because of a sudden disease and now must have dialysis treatments to stay alive. With poor functioning kidneys, the dietitian is presenting all kinds of food restrictions. Rather than tell him what to eat, the dietician provided all kinds of information about how to evaluate what foods to choose given these restrictions.

The restrictions were severe. No milk products, no tomatoes, and no salt, eat foods low in phosphorus, calcium, potassium, no nuts, etc. It also suggested a good balance of protein, and carbohydrates. The protein must be low on bad fats and eat only the carbs from the unrestricted group. The dietitian started him with a suggested list that could be expanded into something more desirable. He studied the new food possibilities with great determination. At first the diet was very bland and unappreciated, but he and his wife began experimenting with healthy foods and foods not often thought of and by adding condiments and spices and proper cooking methods they discovered a surprising amount of tasty foods.

It has been about one year now and he and his wife enjoy eating just as much as they did before. The reason that he was easily able to leave the ice cream, the chocolates, and other goodies was that he was a truly independent person and could make the choices with ease, he also accepted full responsibility for maintaining the best possible continuing health, and, perhaps most importantly, he made the full commitment to a successful program. Fortunately, your problem is not poor kidney function but there is still a question. How do I eat wisely?

From his experience we can conclude that every individual must come to know and understand what goes into their body. This will require that everyone must do what he did—study, learn, and apply what you learned to your own personal menu.

The next part of this chapter will take some time and effort on your part. We know that you will do it because you are an independent, responsible, and committed person. There is a big pay off!

It is impossible to take full responsibility for your eating habits if you don't know what is good or bad. The learning curve is quite high, but the book takes complex ideas and simplifies them so that you will understand. After you master this chapter and move into healthy eating habits, please understand that you have started a life-long process which will improve as you continue the study of good nutrition.

Understanding the System

Understanding the entire food generating process is a formidable challenge. It starts with the original creation of food as a wide variety of chemicals, many questionable, are introduced into the process. Most domestic animals are fed a variety of hormones to induce faster growth and greater bulk. Most grains being produced are laced with various chemicals to spur greater and faster growth and to kill harmful insects. This contamination continues and extends into the food preparation process. Additives are injected into the food to provide a longer shelf life. An overabundance of salt, sugar and other ingredients are added to make food more attractive. While any one of these practices may seem harmless, the composite effect of the entire process can be quite harmful, especially in the long run.

To gain a perspective on this process; remember, our democratic system supports a wide berth for freedom in order to allow for new and innovative ideas. Unfortunately, some of the innovative ideas may need to be more closely monitored to protect the public. In which case, the problem drops right into your lap. Also remember, you are an independent and responsible person and fully capable of monitoring this problem yourself. Certainly, there is steep learning for all of us but the information on how to deal with these problems is out there. Take your responsibility seriously. Read, study, and make decisions based on good information. If you don't do this, you become like a robot that responds to brainwashing and conditioning, questionable advertising, and proper eating habits will disappear.

Suggestions

1. Try to buy organically grown foods. This will be a bit more expensive but the payoff will be great.

2. Use fast food service only occasionally and choose food wisely.

3. Use the Internet and other reading sources to determine what is good or not good for you and respond accordingly. There all kinds of literature available on this matter.

Guidelines for Healthy Food Products

The author, with the help of Rachel Goodwin, a registered dietician, has created the guidelines for you to examine the food items in your current diet. This review will deal mostly with packaged or canned foods as the FDA requires food producers to reveal such information on labels. Because of the variation in the requirements, all of the information listed below may not always appear on all products, but it is a very good start.

Food Label Evaluation Tool

As you go through these next activities, you will be using the *Food Label Evaluation Tool* supplied in Appendix A at the end of this chapter. You will be recording and analyzing your current food list. This will serve as the basis for selecting foods later. You are advised to make a copy of each section in the Appendix. Use that copy to record your research.

You will study the label on each of the various foods that you eat and compare it with the guideline listed below. If a particular product falls well out of range, it is time to make a change from that particular food item. You may not need to change to a different food as food companies often carry different versions. An example might be salt. Most canned soups range quite high in salt but you will find a few that honor a reasonable salt intake. Simply switch to that brand. Let's get at it!

Go now to Appendix A and make a copy of the Food Label Evaluation Tool, Section 1, Daily Caloric Intake.

Calories

The number of calories that one needs each day will vary for everyone, because of body size, physical activity, glandular function, and metabolism rate. Your goals will vary also, for example, eat fewer calories if you want to lose weight, eat a bit more to maintain weight or eat more calories if you want to gain weight.

Use the Internet and you will find any number of daily calorie recommendations for your age, then adjust for your specific goal. An example: the charts suggest that a 40 year old male, six feet tall who exercises moderately will need 2560 calories to maintain weight.

Go now to the Internet and search for calorie intake and find your ideal amount. Start by going to your Internet search engine and typing in *Calories*. Continue searching until you find a chart to help you determine your daily calorie intake.

Record your daily calorie intake in Section 1, *Food Label Evaluation Tool*

Salt

Food processors and cooks tend to lace food with salt to increase its tastiness. Of course, it may sell more food, but at what price? Excess salt in one's system causes the body to retain excess fluids. The heart begins to overwork in order to remove the excess fluid. While this is not a problem in the short run, it can easily lead to later heart problems.

It is not uncommon for canned soup to contain 900 to 1,000 mg of salt, but if you keep looking, you will find some in the 300 to 400 mg range. Always choose a product with the lowest salt content.

Also, be careful of adding more salt to food served to you. The chef will have already introduced the proper amount for you. When you go to a lower salt content in food, the taste difference will be noticeable for a while; food will not seem as tasty. Stick with the lower amounts and your taste buds will gradually adapt. Soon, you will not miss the excess salt at all.

Things you should know about salt:

Canned vegetables such as green beans, corn, and tomatoes have more salt per serving than fresh or frozen vegetables. Canned vegetables have more salt than freshly prepared or frozen vegetables unless you choose foods with "no salt added".

A muffin can have more salt than a bag of potato chips.

Foods can have high salt content and not even taste salty.
Salt is hidden in foods that you might not expect, including salad dressings, cheeses, pasta sauces, breads, tomato juices, and condiments.

Current dietary guidelines for Americans recommend that the general population should consume no more than 2,300 mg of sodium per day (about 1 teaspoon of table salt). (https://www.choosemyplate.gov/2015-2020-dietary-guidelines-answers-your-questions)

1. Excess salt is a main contributor to high blood pressure, negatively affecting the heart.

2. You can lower your salt intake by comparing food labels during shopping and choosing foods lower in salt.

Salt measurements:

½ a teaspoon	=1,500 mg
¾ a teaspoon	=1,725 mg
1 teaspoon	=2,300 mg

Begin your salt intake evaluation by going to the *Food Label Evaluation Tool* and entering the following information. In this part, you will determine the amount of salt (sodium) there is in each of the current foods you eat that has a label. This inspection includes all foods with a label, pantry and refrigerator included.

Study the label on each of the food products that you eat and record the salt content into the evaluation tool for each food item. List your current foods in the left column along with the salt content in **Section 2**.

The information on both Section 2 and Section 2A will be used in making choices for your diet at the end of this chapter.

You are finished with the *Food Label Evaluation Tool* for now. Continue into the next section on sugar.

Sugar

Sugar is beautiful but it is also a two-edged sword. Numerous studies show that sugar, more than any other ingredient in the diet, may be driving some of the world's leading killers including heart disease, diabetes, and even cancer. However sugar is essential. It serves the purpose of giving our bodies the needed strength to support all bodily activity. The danger is getting too much sugar. It is clear adding sugar to what your body needs is completely unnecessary and only adds unwanted calories, thus overweight.

Beside the natural sugar in foods, the food industry adds sugar to many products to make them more appealing, thus leading to the serious health problems. Your goal is to study the food labels carefully and select the foods with the lowest sugar content. Don't be concerned about getting enough sugar a balanced diet will serve you well.

Things you should know about sugar:

> The importance of dealing with the sugar issue is mind boggling. If you use the Internet and type in *sugar the silent killer,* your eyes will be opened. Too much sugar definitely leads to serious health problems.

> It is not uncommon for soft drinks, sweet rolls, doughnuts, cakes, and many other food products to contain 24 or more grams of sugar. A sweet roll, soda, and one other food type would meet your daily requirement. According to one nutrition group the average American consumes 130 pounds of sugar every year.

The American Heart Association recommends the following maximum amounts of sugar:

Men 150 calories per day (37.5 grams or 9 teaspoons)
Women 100 calories per day (25 grams or 6 teaspoons)

According to the USDA's *2015-2020 Dietary Guidelines,* we should limit our total daily consumption of added sugars to less than 10% of calories per day.

There are some great websites that will provide the amount of sugar and other components in food:

www.cwnutritionforbodyandmind.com/sugar-the-silent-killer/
www.medicalnewstoday.com/articles/262978.php
authoritynutrition.com/how-much-sugar-per-day/

It is abundantly clear that you must study your food lists very carefully for sugar content. Keep looking at the various labels on like foods and you will find great variations in sugar content.

You will use the *Food Label Evaluation,* **Section 2,** for this exercise. Most of the food that you eat is already listed in Section 2, so merely enter the sugar amounts in the sugar column, adding any food item to the list that you may have missed.

Potassium

Your body needs potassium to help your muscles contract, maintain fluid balance, and maintain a normal blood pressure. Normal potassium levels in the body help to keep the heart beating regularly. Potassium may help reduce your risk of kidney stones and also bone loss as you age.

Healthy kidneys keep the right amount of potassium in the blood to keep the heart beating at a steady pace. If you have kidney disease, potassium levels can rise and affect your heart. Be sure to talk with your health professional to determine if you should restrict your intake of foods that contain large amounts of potassium.

The USDA recommends adults consume 4,700 mg. of potassium per day. Some good vegetable sources of potassium include sweet potatoes, white potatoes, white beans, tomato products (paste, sauce, and juice), beet greens, soybeans, lima beans, spinach, lentils, and kidney beans. Diets rich in potassium may help to maintain healthy blood pressure.

For the next step you will use your *Food Label Evaluation Tool* **Section 2**. Enter the potassium level in each food item that you eat. Use the table below to help you determine the potassium amounts. You may need to go to the Internet to find any food on your list that is not in the table below. In your search engine, simply type in the specific food, plus "potassium" and you will be able to find the potassium amount for it.

Calcium

Calcium is a mineral. Our bodies contain more calcium than any other mineral. A large percent of the calcium resides in our teeth and bones.

It is essential for building and maintaining our bones. Calcium is also necessary for the function of muscles and blood vessels.

Ages 19-50	1,000 mg each day
Above 50 male	1,000 mg. each day
Above 50 female	1,200 mg each day

(health.gov/dietaryguidelines/2015/guidelines/appendix-7/)

The USDA's ChooseMyPlate.gov website recommends the following:

Choose fat-free or low-fat milk, yogurt, and cheese. If you choose milk or yogurt that is not fat-free or cheese that is not low-fat, the fat in the product counts against your limit of calories from saturated fats.

If sweetened milk products are chosen (flavored milk, yogurt, drinkable yogurt, desserts), the added sugars also count against your limit for calories from added sugar.

For those who are lactose intolerant, smaller portions (such as 4 fluid ounces of milk) may be well tolerated. Lactose-free and lower-lactose products are available. These include lactose-reduced or lactose-free milk, yogurt, and cheese, and calcium-fortified soymilk (soy beverage). Also, enzyme preparations can be added to milk to lower the lactose content.

Calcium choices for those who do not consume dairy products include: kale leaves, calcium-fortified juices, cereals, breads, rice milk, or almond milk.

The amount of calcium that can be absorbed from these foods varies: canned fish (sardines, salmon with bones) soybeans and other soy products (tofu made with calcium sulfate, soy yogurt and tempeh), some other beans, and some leafy greens (collard and turnip greens, kale, bok choy).

Phosphorus

Phosphorus helps to build strong bones, maintains the body pH balance, promotes strong kidneys and helps digestion. Phosphorus and calcium work closely together to build strong bones and teeth.

The recommended daily phosphorus requirement is:

0 to 6 months	100mg per day
7 to 12 months	275 mg per day
1 to 3 years	460 mg per day

4 to 8 years	500 mg per day
9 to 18 years	1,250 mg per day
Adults	700 mg per day

Pregnant or lactating

Younger than 18	1,250 mg per day
Older than 18	700 mg per day

(medlineplus.gov/ency/article/002424.htm)

The U.S. Nation Library of Medicine's MedlinePlus.gov website also states:

> The main food sources are the protein food groups of meat and milk. A diet that includes the right amounts of meal plan calcium and protein will also provide enough phosphorus.

> Whole-grain breads and cereals contain more phosphorus than cereals and breads made from refined flour. However, the phosphorus is stored in a form that is not absorbed by humans. Fruits and vegetables contain only small amounts of phosphorus.

> Phosphorus is readily available in the food supply so deficiency is rare. Excessively high levels of phosphorus in the blood, although rare, can combine with calcium to form deposits in soft tissues such as muscle. High levels of phosphorus in blood only occur in people with severe kidney disease or severe dysfunction of their calcium regulation.

You will use the *Food Label Evaluation*, Section 2 for this exercise. The food that you eat is already listed in Section 2, merely enter the phosphorus amounts in the phosphorus column.

You have now populated your *Food Label Evaluation Tool* with all kinds of great information. This information will be used at the end of the next chapter to build a diet that is right for you.

Understanding Food Groups

A balanced diet is required for us all to have a long, healthy life; thus, we must have some basic knowledge of food groups. Once you have studied and understand this section, you can build a tasty and healthy eating program. Keep in mind that your *real* goal is to become an independent and responsible person, fully capable of meeting all future needs. That demands great health, don't you think?

You will now review the following food groups:

Protein
Carbohydrates
Fat

Protein is the source for building your entire body: bones, muscles, cartilage, skin, and blood. Proteins are also building blocks for enzymes, hormones, and vitamins, enabling strong body functioning.

There are many food choices in the protein group, so as you study the possible menu choices keep in mind that some of the food will contain larger amounts of the bad fats and others larger amounts of the good fats. Even with the steak choices, labels will inform you of the trans fats (bad fats), saturated fats (bad fats), unsaturated fats (good fats), or omega3 fats (good fats). Cheaper processed steaks may contain too much fat, but you can also buy lean cuts. Always make choices that reduce the bad fats.

As you choose your specific food within a food group remember to vary the specific kinds of food. There is an amazing variety, as you will see.

Animal Meat

Start with a lean choice:

The leanest beef cuts include round steaks and roasts (eye of round, top round, bottom round, round tip), top loin, top sirloin, and chuck shoulder and arm roasts.

The leanest pork choices include pork loin, tenderloin, center loin, and ham.

Choose extra lean ground beef. The label should say at least "90% lean." You may be able to find ground beef that is 93% or 95% lean.

Buy skinless chicken parts, or take off the skin before cooking. Remember, skin is a saturated fat (bad).

Boneless skinless chicken breasts and turkey cutlets are the leanest poultry choices.

Choose lean turkey, roast beef, ham, or low-fat luncheon meats for sandwiches instead of luncheon/deli meats with more fat, such as regular bologna or salami.

Keep it lean:

Trim away all of the visible fat from meats and poultry before cooking.

Broil, grill, roast, poach, or boil meat, poultry, or fish instead of frying.

Drain off any fat that appears during cooking.

Skip or limit the breading on meat, poultry, or fish. Breading adds calories. It will also cause the food to soak up more fat during frying.

Prepare beans and peas without added fats and choose and prepare foods without high fat sauces or gravies.

Proteins are found in lesser amounts in many foods, though for most of us, the main source is found in meat and eggs:

beef
chicken
lamb
turkey
pork

Sea Food

Seafood contains a range of nutrients, notably the omega-3 fatty acids, EPA and DHA. Eating about 8 ounces per week of a variety of seafood contributes to the prevention of heart disease. Smaller amounts of seafood are recommended for young children.

Choose seafood (not battered and fried) at least twice a week as the main protein food:

Salmon steak or filet
Salmon loaf
Trout, grilled or baked
Cod
Catfish
Flounder
Haddock
Halibut
Herring
Mackerel
Sea Bass
Snapper
Swordfish
Yellowfin Tuna

Beans, Nuts, and Other Choices

Some recommended meatless dishes:

Chili with kidney or pinto beans
Stir-fried tofu
Split pea, lentil, minestrone, or white bean soups
Baked beans
Black bean enchiladas
Garbanzo or kidney beans on a chef's salad
Rice and beans
Veggie burgers
Hummus (chickpeas) spread on pita bread

Tips for adding protein to dishes, without meat:

Choose unsalted nuts as a snack, on salads, or in main dishes. Use nuts to replace meat or poultry, not in addition to these items:
Use pine nuts in pesto sauce for pasta.
Add slivered almonds to steamed vegetables.
Add toasted peanuts or cashews to a vegetable stir fry instead of meat.
Sprinkle a few nuts on top of low-fat ice cream or frozen yogurt.
Add walnuts or pecans to a green salad instead of cheese or meat.

Helpful Hints in Choosing Proteins

Check the Nutrition Facts label for the saturated fat, *trans* fat, cholesterol, and sodium content of packaged foods (www.choosemyplate.gov/downloads/NutritionFactsLabel.pdf).

Processed meats such as hams, sausages, frankfurters, and luncheon or deli meats have added sodium. Check the ingredient and Nutrition Facts label to help limit sodium intake.

Fresh chicken, turkey, and pork that have been enhanced with a salt-containing solution also have added sodium. Check the product label.

Lower fat versions of many processed meats are available. Look on the Nutrition Facts label to choose products with less trans fat and saturated fat.

To see the protein levels in unlabeled foods, use the *USDA Food Composition Databases* and search for First Nutrient "protein". You can filter your search further by food groups, additional nutrients, etc. (https://ndb.nal.usda.gov/ndb/nutrients/).

Minimum Daily Requirements

Most Americans get enough daily requirements. The problem is to make healthier protein choices. You should get at least 10% of your daily calories, but not more than 35% from protein.

Children	2-3 years old	2 ounce equivalents
	4-8 years old	4 ounce equivalents
Girls	9-13 years old	5 ounce equivalents
	14-18 years old	5 ounce equivalents
Boys	9-13 years old	5 ounce equivalents
	14-18 years old	6 ½ ounce equivalents
Women	19-30 years old	5 ½ ounce equivalents
	31-50 years old	5 ounce equivalents
	51+ years old	5 ounce equivalents
Men	19-30 years old	6 ½ ounce equivalents
	31-50 years old	6 ounce equivalents
	51+ years old	5 ½ ounce equivalents

In general, 1 ounce of meat, poultry or fish, ¼ cup cooked beans, 1 egg, 1 tablespoon of peanut butter, or ½ ounce of nuts or seeds can be considered as 1 ounce-equivalent from the Protein Foods Group. For additional information, including examples of typical ounce-equivalent foods, see https://www.choosemyplate.gov/protein-foods#)

Protein Summary

Go to your *Food Label Evaluation Tool,* Section 3, and begin selecting some of your favorite protein foods that will make up the food choices for all of your meals. Choose a nice variety as you will be making complete menus for your future meals. Be sure to include a variety of fish, meats, beans, and nuts according to the suggestions for getting the correct amount of good fats.

Enter all of these possible choices into your evaluation tool.

Remember to check the fat content before making your final choices. Some of the foods you choose may already be listed in your Section 2. Use that list and include the food items from your protein list. Remember to include a good balance of calcium, phosphorus, and potassium.

Choose only food items that are both low in salt and sugar. This list will be used later to make up the variety of meals to satisfy your diet.

Carbohydrates

Carbohydrates make glucose to fuel the body with energy to function. The body will immediately use the glucose or store an amount not needed.

You can find carbohydrates in the following:

Fruits
Vegetables
Breads, cereals, and other grains
Milk and milk products
Foods containing added sugars (e.g., cakes, cookies, and beverages)

Healthier foods higher in carbohydrates include ones that provide dietary fiber and whole grains as well as those without added sugars.

Some diet books use "bad" carbs when referring to foods with refined carbohydrates, meaning they are made from white flour and added sugars. Examples include white bread, cakes, and cookies. Avoid choosing these foods.

"Good" carbs describe foods that have more fiber and complex carbohydrates. Complex carbohydrates are carbohydrates that take longer to break down into glucose; such as vegetables, fruits, whole grains and beans.

There are two main types of carbohydrates:

Complex carbohydrates
Simple carbohydrates

Complex Carbohydrates

Starch and dietary fiber are the two types of complex carbohydrates. Starch must be broken down through digestion before your body can use it as a glucose source.

Quite a few foods contain starch and dietary fiber such as breads, cereals, and vegetables:

Starch is in certain vegetables (i.e., potatoes, dry beans, peas, and corn).
Starch is also found in breads, cereals, and grains.
Dietary fiber is in vegetables, fruits, and whole grain.

Choose complex carbohydrates as they will take longer to produce energy thus providing continuous energy for a sustained period. Simple carbs, coming from sugar based products tend to spike immediately after eating. That is, you will get a sudden burst of energy but it will fall off quickly.

Carbohydrate Intake

According to the USDA's health.gov website, adults should get 45 percent to 65 percent of their calories from carbohydrates. One of your problems will be to avoid simple sugars. So much of our food is laced heavily with sugar. If you don't pay attention to the amounts of sugar in the food you eat, you will likely be getting way more sugar than is healthy. When filling out the next section of the *Food Label Evaluation Tool,* avoid foods that are high in sugar.

Go to your *Food Label Evaluation Tool* **Section 4** and make a long list of food items from the carbohydrate group to include on your daily menus. Be sure to use a great variety. The foods that you are building into your program will end up to be a very long list of possible foods that will be great for your health. Keep working, and this process will come together in a beautiful way at the finish. Remember, many of the foods that you select may be listed in **Section 2** of the *Food Label Evaluation Tool.* Use that list and include the food items you would like onto your protein list. Remember to include a good balance of calcium, phosphorus, and potassium. Choose only food items that are both low in salt and sugar.

Dietary Fiber

Dietary fiber or roughage is the indigestible portion of food derived from plants. It has two main components, soluble fiber, which dissolves in water quickly, and insoluble fiber, which does not dissolve in water, is metabolically inert and provides bulking. Too much of one or the other will lead to constipation or diarrhea.

Just like a street sweeper goes through your neighborhood picking up rubbish in the gutter, insoluble fiber sweeps through your gut, pushing waste along. It helps you have regular bowel movements.

How much fiber do we need? Women need 25 grams of fiber per day and men need 38 grams per day. Current studies show that most people eat only about 15 grams per day. Please do not become one of these people

Fruits and vegetables are a good source of fiber:

> Lettuce, Swiss chard, raw carrots, and spinach
> Tender cooked vegetables, such as asparagus, beets, mushrooms, turnips, and pumpkin

Baked potatoes and sweet potatoes with skin
Broccoli, artichokes, squashes, and string beans
Vegetable smoothies
Legumes, such as lentils, black beans, split peas, kidney beans, lima beans, and chickpeas
Nuts and seeds, such as sunflower seeds, almonds, pistachios, and pecans
Apples and bananas
Peaches and pears
Tangerines, prunes, and berries
Figs and other dried fruits

Grains are another important source of dietary fiber:

Hot cereals, such as oatmeal and farina (Cream of Wheat)
Whole-grain breads
Brown rice
Popcorn
High-fiber cereals, such as bran, shredded wheat, Grape Nuts, Ry Krisp, and puffed wheat
Whole-wheat pastas
Bran muffins

(https://medlineplus.gov/ency/patientinstructions/000193.htm)

Fats

Fact: People often have a skewed view of the role of fats in their diet. In reality some fats are not good but others are.

Fact: Trans fats and saturated fats are not good for you in that they will increase your risk for heart disease and cause excess weight gain.

Fact: Mono-unsaturated fats and polyunsaturated fats are known as the "good fats" because they are good for your heart and overall health.

https://medlineplus.gov/ency/patientinstructions/000104.htm

Good Fats

Mono-unsaturated fat	*Polyunsaturated fat*
Olive oil	Grapeseed oil
Canola oil	Corn oil

Sunflower oil	Safflower oil
Peanut oil	Walnuts
Safflower oil	Sunflower
Sesame oil	Sesame seeds
Avocados	Flaxseed
Soybean oil	fatty fish
Peanut butter	Soybean oil

Bad Fats

High in Saturated Fats	*High in Trans Fats*
high-fat cuts of meat	doughnuts and muffins
chicken with the skin	sweet rolls
butter	microwave popcorn
cheese	crackers
poultry with skin	chips
ice cream	anything battered & fried
milk	stick margarine
lard	pie and pie crust
Palm oil	non-dairy creamer
Coconut oil	frozen dinners
candy bars	cake mixes and frosting
	candy bars

The above lists are recommended by registered dietician, Rachel Goodwin.

Regarding the above list of bad fats, it is not necessary to eliminate all of them from your food list. You may eat red meat, but buy lean meat. You may eat chicken, but remove the skin. Limited cheese and butter are fine. The way in which you cook the bad fats makes a difference. Try to grill or bake rather than fry. For all foods, read the nutrition labels.

Try to eliminate trans fats from your diet. Check food labels for trans fats. Avoiding commercially-baked goods goes a long way. Also limit fast food.

Limit your intake of saturated fats by cutting back on red meat and full-fat dairy foods. Try replacing red meat with beans, nuts, poultry, and fish whenever possible, and switching from whole milk and other full-fat dairy foods to lower fat versions.

Eat omega-3 fats every day. Good sources include fish, walnuts, ground flax seeds, flaxseed oil, canola oil, and soybean oil.

Go to your *Food Label Evaluation Tool* **Section 5,** and using the above information, enter the good fats you will want to eat in the column headed *Food Items.* Put a checkmark in the column that identifies the type of fat. Be sure to go through the list of foods generated in Section 2. Use that list and include the food items you would like onto your protein list. Remember to include a good balance of calcium, phosphorus, and potassium. Choose only food items that are both low in salt and sugar.

Cholesterol

Cholesterol is created naturally by the body and is essential for good health. Including too much bad fat in your diet will raise the cholesterol levels and cause a fat build up in the arteries, eventually causing blood-flow blockage and a possible heart attack. It is important to monitor the cholesterol levels in your body by getting a blood test.

Total cholesterol is a measure of this special fat created naturally by the body. The current guidelines say that a person's cholesterol should be 200 or below. A blood test will show your number.

Low Density Lipoprotein (LDL) is a component of the total cholesterol and is the enemy that can cause plaque buildup in the arteries.

High Density Lipoprotein (HDL) is a second component of the total cholesterol and is a friend to help keep your body strong.

The goal is to try and keep the LDL low and the HDL high. Again, a blood test will provide the needed numbers. The general guidelines are:

total cholesterol	200 or less
LDL	100 or less
HDL	40-59 the higher the better

(medlineplus.gov/magazine/issues/summer12/articles/summer12pg6-7.html)

This is a matter of diet, but it is also about life style. Here are suggested ways to lower cholesterol:

    limiting alcohol intake
    decreasing caloric intake
    avoiding foods high in trans fats acid and LDL cholesterol
    losing weight
    quitting smoking
    exercising
    adding soluble fiber and omega-3 fatty acids to your diet

(medlineplus.gov/magazine/issues/summer12/articles/summer12pg6-7.html)

Vitamins

Vitamin supplements are no substitute for a healthy diet, but nobody's perfect when it comes to healthful eating. It can be particularly challenging to get the nutrients you need if you are on a restricted diet or if you avoid animal or dairy products. Some of us take a daily multivitamin as nutritional insurance. The truth is, if you do a good job planning your eating needs, there will be no need for vitamin supplements. If for some reason a doctor might restrict you from eating certain foods, it would be necessary to find the vitamins needed for that particular case. Your doctor will advise you and you can also conduct Internet research to learn what your specific needs are.

Take note that vitamin supplements, taken in excess, can be dangerous. Also some vitamins can conflict with others, either degrading their effects or magnifying them unpredictably. Proceed with the assistance of your doctor or nutritionist, when selecting vitamins.

Continue using the Internet to learn more about vitamin advantages and pitfalls and you will be prepared to make the right choices when needed.

Putting it All Together

I hope that you have digested the information presented. It is basic and must be understood in your mind and at all times. You cannot do what is correct if you don't have the right information. Now comes the time when you will complete the work. It will demand much from you but the pay-off is great.

Finding Healthier Foods

You now have a complete listing of the foods that you eat with important information about each food product on the **Section 2** list. Take the Section 2 list with you and go to your favorite grocery store. Also take a copy of **Section 2A** in the Appendix to record your research at the grocery store.

Next, you will gather more information about the foods on the Section 2 list from the grocery store. Locate the first food item from your Section 2 list in the grocery store and compare the information on that food item with the one on your Section 2 list. Continue looking for the same food item and locate the one that is lowest in salt, sugar and medium in calcium, potassium and phosphorus. Once you locate that food, enter it into food list Section 2A.

Continue this same process until you have covered all food items. This may take more than one visit to the store.

Wa-la! You have a listing of foods that are most healthy.

Your Complete Food List

All of the hard work that you have been doing will now really payoff. Your goal is to translate the long food lists that you have included in the three food groups into tasty recommended meals. To begin, you will select the foods that you think would provide a nice variety of breakfast meals. The Food Planning List at the end of this chapter contains pages that will help you make these choices and provide a place to record the choices to create a breakfast menu.

Most people who have very successful diets tend to stick with certain choices rather than jump all over the place with too many choices. At the start of your program, it is better to provide more choices than you might use one year from now. The reasoning is that in the beginning, you won't be certain of what might become your favorite choices. By allowing four or more meal choices, you can experiment with various breakfast meals. You will gradually learn to appreciate certain meals.

Having completed your breakfast menus, you will do the same for lunch and dinner. Locate **Section** 1, breakfast Section **2,** lunch and **Section 3,** dinner at the end of this chapter and make blank copies for the work.

Remember to watch the calorie count of each food and try to stay within it as you make food choices. Many labels will display the calories. If you are not sure of the calories in certain foods, find a good food calorie list by using the web to locate the topic and type in: food calorie count.

In your search for more information, consider going to your local book store and browse for a good book on nutrition to fill in gaps in your knowledge. A good book will likely have food lists their calorie count.

Starting Your New Eating Program

Now that you have a great plan for healthy eating, it is likely necessary for you to do several things. First, go into your pantry and refrigerator and begin tossing out those negative foods that you will eliminate from your eating program. Second, if you have not done so already, make your shopping list to include those new and healthy foods that appear on your many food menus. Now you are all set to accomplish one of your dreams—great health!

Remember to vary the meals listed on your menus and to try different combinations of food that pleases you.

Final Thought

Congratulations on coming this far. It is obvious that you have the staying power to be this independent person, willing and able to take full charge of all of your responsibilities. Let this special power roll into all of the other demands in your life, for this is the way to live a quality life. Never allow yourself to slip back into a thoughtless way of living.

Congratulations Captain.

Food Label Evaluation Tools

This tool is used to gather information about what constitutes good eating habits. You will gather information about the foods that you eat or would like to eat. Then you will use this same information to build a tasty, balanced, and healthy food program for yourself.

Section 1 - Daily Caloric Intake

Enter the calories that your body needs each day_____

Section 2 - Content of Salt Sugar Potassium Calcium and Phosphorus-Your Pantry

Food Item	Brand Name	mg Salt	mg Sugar	mg Potassium	mg Calcium	mg Phosphorus

Section 2 Table Continued

Food Item	Brand Name	mg Salt	mg Sugar	mg Potassium	mg Calcium	mg Phosphorus

Section 2A - Searching Store Products

Your job is to locate foods that are low and medium low in each of the categories salt and sugar and medium in potassium, calcium and phosphorus. Using your food list from Section 2 as a guide, locate the same food items on the store shelf and record the ones that have low and medium low mg values. One item may be low in some areas and high in others. Omit the ones where a category may be high. Your goal is to create a new food health list to include in your food choices.

Food Item	Brand Names	mg Salt	mg Sugar	mg Potassium	mg Calcium	mg Phosphrous

Section 2A Continued

Food Item	Brand Names	mg Salt	mg Sugar	mg Potassium	mg Calcium	mg Phosphrous

Section 3 – Protein Table

Food Item Protein	Name Brand	Saturated Fat	Trans Fat	Polyunsaturated Fat	Monounsaturated Fat

Section 3 Protein Table Continued

Food Item Protein	Name Brand	Saturated Fat	Trans Fat	Polyunsaturated Fat	Monounsaturated Fat

Section 4 – Carbohydrate Table

Food Item Carbohydrates	Brand Name	Soluble	Insoluble	Carbs		

Section 4 – Carbohydrate Table Continued

Food Item Carbohydrates	Brand Name	Soluble	Insoluble	Carbs		

Section 5 – Fat Table

Food Item Fat	Name Brand	Monounsaturated Fat	Polyunsaturated Fat	Saturated Fats	Trans Fats

Section 5 – Fat Table Continued

Meal Planning

Breakfast Meals - Section 1

Using your food lists from Sections 3, 4, and 5, choose foods to make up complete breakfast meals, being certain to include a good balance of protein, carbohydrates, and fats. Here are reminders of daily intake of each food group regarding balance and caloric intake for the day. Transfer your daily calorie intake from, Section 1, page 64. Choose only the number of breakfast meals that you like. It is not necessary to create exactly six meals. If you want more than six, make an additional copy of this page.

Calorie intake:_____

Daily intake of Protein:_____

Daily intake of Carbohydrates:_____

Daily intake of Fats:_____

Breakfast 1	Breakfast 2	Breakfast 3	Breakfast 4	Breakfast 5	Breakfast 6

Lunch Meals – Section 2

Using your food lists from Sections 3, 4, and 5, choose foods to make up complete lunch meals, being certain to include a good balance of protein, carbohydrates, and fats. Here are reminders of daily intake of each food group regarding balance and caloric intake for the day. Transfer your daily calorie intake from Section 1, page 64. Choose only the number of lunch meals that you like. It is not necessary to create exactly six meals. If you want more than six, make an additional copy of this page.

Calorie intake:_____

Daily intake of Protein:_____

Daily intake of Carbohydrates:_____

Daily intake of Fats:_____

Lunch Meals 1	Lunch Meals 2	Lunch Meals 3	Lunch Meals 4	Lunch Meals 5	Lunch Meals 6

Dinner Meals – Section 3

Using your food lists from Sections 3, 4, and 5, choose foods to make up a complete dinner meals, being certain to include a good balance of protein, carbohydrates, and fats. Here are reminders of daily intake of each food group regarding balance and caloric intake for the day. Transfer your daily calorie intake from Section 1, page 64. Choose only the number of dinner meals that you like. It is not necessary to create exactly six meals. If you want more than six, make an additional copy of this page.

Calorie intake:_____

Daily intake of Protein:_____

Daily intake of Carbohydrates:_____

Daily intake of Fats:_____

Dinner Meals 1	Dinner Meals 2	Dinner Meals 3	Dinner Meals 4	Dinner Meals 5	Dinner Meals 6

Refer to the next page see the food daily requirement list.

Additional Nutrition Studies

The information presented in this chapter is basic and must be understood to eat properly. Understanding good eating habits will take continued learning throughout your life. If you wish to go a bit deeper at this time, the author has included a number of websites that he found useful and so you may continue your nutrition education now.

Nutrition Websites

A study of these websites will expand your understanding of nutrition.
http://www.hsph.harvard.edu/nutritionsource
http://www.bodybuilding.com/content/ultimate-list-40-high-protein-foods.html
https://www.verywell.com/what-is-dietary-fat-3496105
http://www.webmd.com/food-recipes/guide/grocery-list#1
http://www.webmd.com/diet/food-fitness-planner/default.htm
https://www.choosemyplate.gov/protein-foods#
https://medlineplus.gov/dietaryfiber.html
https://health.gov/dietaryguidelines/2015/guidelines/
http://www.nutrition.gov

CHAPTER FOUR

Fitness through Exercise

Congratulations for joining us on this wonderful journey to physical fitness. We live in such a wonderful world of automation with gadgets of every kind to do most of the physical labor that we did in years past. That's a great thing but—it seems to limit our physical activity and there is not much time left to exercise at the gym. This in a nut shell is the dilemma of the majority of Americans resulting in serious problems with obesity, weak heart, clogged arteries, diabetes, breathing problems, bad back, and many other maladies.

The evidence gathered from testing, clearly shows that proper physical exercise is the major answer to staving off these really serious health issues, allowing people to live long and prosperous lives while feeling really good and keeping medical costs at a minimum. The price that you must pay for good health is—taking the time and doing what your body needs.

I know that this will not be a problem for you, why? You have already proven that you are an *independent, responsible, committed* person. Decide right this minute to take full responsibility for keeping healthy. All that remains is for you to study the problem, choose those activities that will give you great health, and make the commitment to follow through with absolute perfection.

HealthierUS.gov defines physical activity as *any form of exercise or movement of the body that uses energy.* Some of your daily life activities—doing active chores around the house, yard work, walking the dog—are examples. To get the health benefits of physical activity, include activities that make you breathe harder and make your heart and blood vessels healthier. These aerobic activities include things like brisk walking, running, dancing, swimming, and playing basketball. Also include strengthening activities to make your muscles stronger, like push-ups and lifting weights.

Before diving into an exercise program, let's expand our perspective of the health issues to understand all of the benefits. That way you are not apt to leave out necessary activities in your program.

Many studies point out the amazing benefits of exercise to our cardiovascular system. It is recommended that those seeking good heart and vascular health maintain moderate-intensity activity. The heart is a muscle and must be maintained as any muscle. Half of our exercise program should consist of aerobic activities including walking, jogging, bicycling, swimming, boat rowing, stationary bike, and other devices that require continued application to the point of creating some oxygen debt. The other half of the program will be strength training. The vascular system is enhanced as exercise causes the blood to flow faster within the vessels and arteries thus expanding them to keep them flexible. Additionally, it keeps blood flowing well through our various body organs, muscles and bones are improved.

There is evidence to show that moderate exercise has beneficial effects on the immune system.

Moderate exercise has been associated with a 29% decrease incidence of upper respiratory tract infection.

According to healthypeople.gov, studies show exercise can lower the risk of:

- Early death
- Coronary heart disease
- Stroke
- High blood pressure
- Type 2 diabetes
- Breast and colon cancer
- Falls
- Depression

Among children and adolescents, physical activity can:

- Improve bone health.
- Improve cardiorespiratory and muscular fitness.
- Decrease levels of body fat.
- Reduce symptoms of depression.

For people who are inactive, even small increases in physical activity are associated with health benefits.

Muscle and Skeletal System

Muscles are what move the human body. A total of 700 muscles are attached to the bones in the body and account for about half of one's body weight. Muscles seldom work alone; rather, they work in groups to accomplish body movement. Muscles are also responsible to maintain good body posture.

The program that you choose will be most likely to maintain your muscle groups and strengthen them. You may wish to hike down the Grand Canyon, for example.

The skeleton has six major roles: supporting movement, protecting vital organs, producing blood cells, storing minerals and regulating the endocrine system. The average person reaches maximum bone density at age 30, after that there is a slow deterioration of bone mass. This simply means that we must pay close attention to keeping our bones strong for a lifetime. We realize that proper diet has much to do with bone mass but many are unaware that exercise strengthens the bones.

Are you willing to take on this responsibility?

Surprisingly, the number one reason people ignore good health habits is apathy; just taking it for granted that we can maintain good health regardless of what we eat or how we exercise. Yes, we seem to easily get by through our 20's and 30's but in our 40's and 50's we begin to see some serious tell tails. Suddenly, a problem pops up. Perhaps overweight to the point of making it very difficult to return to normal. One's immune system may have been compromised leading to far too much illness like flu, colds, and other ailments.

And sadly, poor habits over 20 years may have damaged one of the vital organs. For some problems, it may be too late, but in most cases a person can jump on the good health band wagon and reverse many of the problems. Don't wait any longer. Join us now and revitalize your whole being. If you are already struggling with serious issues, you have no choice but follow doctor's orders and join us. Start now, no matter what age.

Aerobic Exercise

Aerobic exercise is accomplished by a sustained, continuous activity that causes the heart to beat faster and creates oxygen debt. This exercising requires at least 20 minutes up to an hour or more, depending on one's level of fitness and goals. Aerobic exercise should be maintained at least three days each week up to exercising every day. This will depend upon your current level of fitness and your goals.

Before starting any exercise, let us consider some special thoughts. Most people will get the greatest benefit and lower their risks if they keep their heart rate between 50% and 85% of their maximum heart rate when exercising. The figures below are averages, so use them as general guidelines.

Age	*Target HR Zone 50-85%*	*Average Maximum Heart Rate, 100%*
20 years	100-150 beats per minute	200 beats per minute
30 years	95-142 beats per minute	190 beats per minute
40 years	90-135 beats per minute	180 beats per minute

50 years	85-127 beats per minute	170 beats per minute
60 years	80-120 beats per minute	160 beats per minute
70 years	75-113 beats per minute	150 beats per minute

(http://www.nhlbi.nih.gov/health/resources/heart/obesity-guide-physical-active-html#tc22)

Important note: a few high blood pressure medications lower the maximum heart rate and thus the target zone rate. If you're taking such medicine, call your physician to find out if you need to use a lower target heart rate.

Alternately, to precisely figure out your maximum heart rate, subtract your age (in years) from 220. This number is your maximum heart rate. To figure out your target heart rate range, multiply that number by 0.50 and 0.85.

For example, if you are 40 years of age, subtract 40 from 220 to get your maximum heartrate of 180 beats per minute (220 - 40 = 180). Then, multiply 180 by 0.50 and 0.85 to get your target heart rate range of 90 to 153 beats per minute (180 x 0.50 = 90 and 180 x 0.85 = 153). When you first start an exercise program, aim for the lower end of your target heart rate range. As your exercise program progresses, you can gradually build up to a higher target heart rate.

The above rule is a general rule for easy use. You can go to the web and locate a heart-rate calculator to find your exact level for your age and physical condition. In your search engine type in: heart rate calculator.

This kind of activity can easily be accomplished at home or at a fitness center, or both. Let's study the possibilities for exercise at your home.

Fitness at Home

Walking is as natural as anything we do. Just step it up and move into your neighborhood with some brisk walking. Ideally, you may find a park nearby as walking on grass is quite beneficial to the knees. Be sure that you have a good pair of walking shoes. Plan a route that will last 30 minutes and head out. Walk vigorously enough where you need to step up breathing and maintain that comfortable pace for the full 30 minutes. If you can handle a bit more speed, do so, but taking care to slow down if breathing becomes labored. As the days go by, increase your walking time a few minutes each week and aim for 45 minutes to 1 hour for each session. When you feel strong enough, extend the time as you wish. Soon you will be ready to hit one of the local hiking trails.

Running or jogging follows the same pattern as walking, just step up the pace. The advantage is that you will burn more calories than walking during the same time period. Running for 30 minutes should cover about 2 1/2 miles or more. As you gain strength, increase your running time until you run for 45 minutes to 1 hour each day.

Cycling, riding your own bicycle is another matter and must be carefully considered. If you don't already have a bicycle, you will need to consider the expense of a bike, clothing, helmet and proper shoes. If you have a bicycle and want to gain health using it, you must give it careful thought.

Ideally, you live in an area that has well defined bike paths. This, of course, is safer than riding in the road. Look for a route on streets that are less traveled and be certain that you have a good rear-view mirror and reflective clothing. Distances will vary considerably depending on the type of bike you are using and your physical condition.

The goal is to increase breathing activity to create some oxygen debt. Use time as your guide and begin by riding 30 minutes each day, increasing each week during the next two months. Learn to enjoy the ride and see the sights.

Swimming is a great way to go. There are public and private pools available all year long. Just as in walking or running, swim your laps, creating some oxygen debt and maintain for 30 minutes or longer. Increase the time for swimming over the next two months to 45 minutes to an hour. Swim three to seven days each week.

The great advantage of swimming is that it is far easier on the body than walking or running. It removes that jarring effect to the body. The author varied his program by running, swimming, and hiking. It was nice to break up the activity.

Pay attention to your body. Stop exercising if you feel very out of breath, dizzy, faint, or nauseous, or if you feel pain. Talk with your family doctor if you have questions or think you have injured yourself.

Exercise—Home or the Gym

Exercising at home is great because you can do it at any time. You might consider capturing a corner of one room for exercising. The author has done that by putting down a half inch rubber mat for sitting or lying down exercises.

There are many exercise devices that are inexpensive and work well. Some will include good size machines used to exercise various body parts made for the home. These devices are somewhat expensive and require considerable space. There are many other inexpensive devices that will work for you.

Investigate the possibility of adding these items to your home gym.

Rubber resistance devices are thick strands of rubber tubing with handles on each end. Hook them to a door knob or hook and pull in various ways to build strength. They are easy to use and inexpensive.

Small dumbbells are very useful and inexpensive.

A medicine ball is used to toss back and forth with a partner.

Foam rollers are used for therapeutic exercises.

Stability ball is used to sit on or lie on and move to gain strength and stability.

You can go on-line and find a variety of items but it is best to visit a sporting goods store where you can see these items and have a clerk help you. The best advice I can give is don't be too quick to buy an expensive exercise machine, especially if you are just starting. Get started with the items listed and go from there as you need.

Aerobic Fitness in the Gym

Most gyms will have all kinds of aerobic devices that work effectively. The most common one is the treadmill. This machine provides a walking surface that moves at whatever pace one chooses to set. Additionally, the user can raise or lower the walking surface to simulate hills. The great advantages are that the walking surface is made to be easier on the knees than concrete and you are not required to walk in traffic. The disadvantage is that you won't get to see the sights along the way. You will also find a number of walking devices in the gym to simulate walking or running, including stationery bicycles.

What is Strength Training?

Strength training is exercise that develops the strength and endurance of large muscle groups. It is also called "resistance training" or "weight training." Lifting weights is an example of this type of exercise. Exercise machines can provide strength training. Push-ups, pull-ups, sit-ups, and leg squats are also strength-training exercises.

The trainer at a gym can give you more information about exercising safely with weights or machines. If you have high blood pressure or other health problems, be sure to talk to your family doctor before beginning strength training.

Warm-up and cool-down stretches

Before starting either aerobic or anaerobic exercise, take time to do some stretches. Touch your toes, bend side to side, twist your torso, and stretch your legs. By doing stretches, you will reduce the possibility of muscle damage.

When performing any of the stretches described below, keep the following in mind:

> Keep your breathing slow and natural. Do not hold your breath.
> Move slowly and steadily. Avoid jerky movements to prevent injury.
> Do not bounce while stretching. Bouncing can cause muscles to tear.

Anaerobic Fitness at the Gym

For developing a strength fitness program, it is recommended that you consider joining a fitness center near you or joining the YMCA. Most of these gyms will have a great variety of equipment, including both weights and exercise machines. The best part is that you will also receive help in using the equipment and you may also, for a minimal fee, hire a private trainer to get you started and to maintain your exercise program.

A gym will often have a swimming pool and will offer water aerobics. Hot baths and sauna baths are usually available at most gyms.

If you are not certain about how to go about getting started, go to your local bookstore and find a good book on becoming physically fit. You should also use the Internet—do so by typing *exercise* into your browser. You will find more information than you want.

Final Notes

The great part about an exercise program is that it is right at your finger-tips. All you need to do is step out of the house and start walking or running. I'm sure that you already know the biggest problem—just taking time to do it and stick with it. I know that problem is no longer with you for you are independent, responsible, and committed to your beliefs. Keep it going, the rest of your life. I am in my 80s, exercise faithfully and maintain the same weight that I was during my senior year of high school.

Assignment

1. Sit down with pencil and paper (and with a significant other if you have one) and plan the time when you will start walking or jogging.

2. Determine the best route and the length of time you will exercise.

3. Decide on anything you need to buy, such as good shoes or running clothes, perhaps a stop watch.

4. Step out the door and GO.

5. As you move along with the walking or running, add whatever exercise experiences you feel will help you most.

6. Continue faithfully for the rest of your life.

Keep it going, and one day you will come to look forward to it every day—and you'll love it!

Good sailing, Captain.

Websites on Physical Fitness

www.wikihow.com/Get-Fit
www.active.com/fitness/articles/tips-for-getting-physically-fit
www.medicalnewstoday.com/articles/7181.php#cardiorespiratory_endurance
www.livestrong.com/article/501546-5-ways-to-stay-physically-fit/
www.presidentschallenge.org/motivated/ten-ideas.shtml

CHAPTER FIVE

Keeping Mentally Strong

As children we are nurtured by parents and the community to grow and become a successful participant in life. Each one of us is a unique being living our lives using the sum total of our experience, with many differences and many similarities. It is this diversity that provides fuel for the many great opportunities to live in a rich and comfortable environment. The inventors, artists, seers, developers, doers, planners have created an unbelievable world. Yet in all of this, we seem to take life for granted and live it without much thought to our individual uniqueness. Our goal in this section of the book is to help you become aware of the untapped possibilities that lie within.

The untapped power of the mind is staggering. We look at Mozart, who at the age of six years old was writing symphonies and directing major orchestras, Einstein with his unbelievable mathematical skills, Da Vinci with his paintings and visions of things to come. We hold all of these people in highest esteem, feeling that this is only something for the special, saintly people.

Is it only for special people? No, after teaching thousands of students of all ages for over 40 years, I conclude that everyone has the potential for uncommon success. Why is it that some of our students go on to become company presidents, college presidents, senators, great athletes, authors, great painters…? What is even more unbelievable is that many of these students came to us with the appearance that success would be hard to come by. I recall a young woman riding into the college parking lot on a motorcycle, a bit rough-hewn but with the notion that there was something better for her life here. The transformation of this girl to a beautiful young woman was remarkable—today she remains a good friend and is a college professor.

Another story that convinced me there is hope for everyone is about a young man who came to my office with an unusual presentation. I was the director of computer technology at my college , helping teachers use computer technology to help students learn. He informed me that he was a college student and computer technician at a different college and had heard about the high level of success we were enjoying. He told me that he knew we were on the right track and wanted to join our technical staff.

No doubt about it he was a skilled and able programmer and technician, but it was also clear that he would bring considerable serious emotional baggage into the mix. It would be a tough call but something inside my being told me that this was a special opportunity. He went into our *Innovation Center* where he would meet with faculty and develop the dream that would improve learning opportunities for students using technology. With the young man there, the creative ideas flowed and a number of very innovative learning systems were developed with great success.

We were also able to help him with his emotional baggage and he became quite functional. It was clear after several years that he had outgrown his job so we arranged an interview for him with one of the major educational software companies. He got the job—today he is a top executive and one of five team leaders, each responsible for one product. His product consistently out sells the other four products.

What is amazing about this story is that the young man was so busy with his work that he was not able to finish his degree. So there he is—no degree, but a top corporate job. What does that tell you?

Yes, it is true. Every one of you has unlimited potential, in fact, the only real limitations are the ones we put on ourselves. You've heard it before, "there is no way I can do that." But there is!

Let's begin with the idea that you must become an innovator. Innovation plays an essential role, for it is the only way to improve the human condition. Here is my definition of an innovator:

An innovator is a person able to dream the dream but also has the ability to make the dream come true. There is quite a lot implied in this statement. The beginning point is *awareness*. You must become aware of both the need and your possible involvement with satisfying that need before anything can happen.

Back in the 1960's I was teaching college business subjects and knew that computers would have a continuing impact on learning, so I studied programing and used the mainframe computer to help with my classes. It worked quite well with the statistics and math classes.

In the late 1970's the microcomputer was born and I knew that there would be an unbelievable explosion of computer usage. My college was perplexed and confused about how to use the devices with many departments each asking for their own lab to do so many different tasks. It was clear to me that this route would lead to disaster. We would end up with a mishmash of operating systems and wiring schemes, fully unable to furnish the required technical support in each separate lab. What we desperately needed was a common infrastructure with a central software library that would furnish all of the microcomputers needed for all segments of the college all centralized in one place.

It took about one week to complete the details for the dream plan. My solution was to build one large area in which to place all of the various computers, all connected to a shared network. A software library would be maintained in the building so that any software was available to any user. Further, there would be a special group made up of faculty members, technicians, and teaching assistants working in the center during all open hours. It would run much like a library. Computers would be available seven days a week for any student or faculty member.

Most departments in the college rejected the plan as they each wanted to control their own lab, not realizing the difficulties that it meant for them. I approached the instructional deans and the president with my idea and it made sense to several administrators and they loved the idea as it would be financially feasible and would provide computers for all departments. All faculty and all students would have access to them. My idea was to envision the computer learning center much like a library. Expert personnel would be hired to assist faculty as they used the computers and tutoring aid to students.

The idea was accepted and I knew that it was a perfect plan to receive a grant. No such learning lab existed in the country. We wrote, won the grant and received enough money to run the center for two years, costing the college nothing. The prototype was so successful that millions of dollars of bond money was given over to the project. The college built a new learning center with a 9,000 square-foot room that housed 365 computers. Specialized computer classrooms were built around the perimeter of the area to teach computer systems and languages. During the first two years of operations there were 2,000 tours from people all over the world who came to see and learn how to duplicate the same success for themselves. Our 9,000 square foot learning area was dubbed the largest classroom in the world.

I tell you this story not because of its interest but to show you that one person in the right place, with the right idea, who is willing to step out of the box, can make a huge impact. Please—know there are no limitations except that which is perceived.

Why do I feel so strongly about the need to innovate? Because everything that you do in this life can likely be improved upon, be it managing a family, improving your job skills, improving your knowledge, your social life or anything else that you must do. This will not happen without stepping out of the box for that is where new ideas begin. There must be a desire in all that we do to do things better. Wouldn't you like to improve your job skills in hopes of receiving more pay and do more challenging work? Wouldn't you like to find more time to spend with your spouse and children? It really makes little difference whether the innovation is big like building a high-tech learning center or finding a better way to redo your budget dollars enabling the best use of money.

If you were successful in changing to healthy eating habits using this book, you have already enjoyed the process of innovation. You must think outside of what you deem as normal and be willing to investigate what is possible. Each of you is engaged in a whole host of life activities which vary considerably. Your challenges will vary accordingly, so each of you must look at the areas of your life that are not really acceptable for you and your family.

I'll cite a great example for you. I met a couple in their late 40s' that had purchased a home in 2008, just before a major recession. The drop-in home prices did not bother them for they knew the prices would recover one day. That was fine until a serious problem arose. The husband was diagnosed with diabetes and soon his lower-left leg and part of his right foot were amputated. He was a large man and the wheel chair would not fit through the doors of his home and worse yet, the bedrooms and family office were upstairs. The bathrooms were too small. The doors could be widened at great expense but getting upstairs was another matter.

Their current home mortgage was now about equal to the sales value meaning that there was little or no equity. If they sold now, they could not recover any equity at all. Because of the recent high cost for medical care, their budget was blown away and there was very little cash available.

Why not just buy a new house and secure a mortgage? A new house built to cover medical issues was quite expensive and very little cash was available resulting in a very high mortgage payment. There was no answer to the standard way to solve the problem.

They began to look for a house that needed repair hoping they could build the wheelchair ramps and make the home medically friendly. It took about six months before they found a good possibility. While the house was run down more than they wanted, it meant the price for the house was quite low.

During the time of their searches, they met and befriended a young man just starting a construction company who agreed to do any remodeling work for the cost of buying product and would add no profit. The contractor would bill them for his time only, reducing remodeling costs about 40%. He viewed this as a start-up job for his company.

That was all fine, but they needed cash to pay for the house and more cash for the redo. Yes, the final result would be great in terms of total cash outlay, but how do they buy the house. As they were seeking advice on what to do from another friend, an interesting thing happened. The gentleman was as financially generous as he was financially endowed and offered to provide the cash for the redo. The house was slated to be ready in four months. At the same time, they started the process of securing a new mortgage so that the construction mortgage from their friend could be paid off in four months. The couple ended up with a lovely medically friendly home for slightly less than $300,000. The appraisal from the bank came in $350,000. It appears that they already have $50,000 worth of equity in the house. Imagine what innovation can do for you. All that happened because they were able to think outside the box.

Summary on Innovation

To innovate is to break new ground. Become an innovator and you accomplish things that others only dream about. The process of innovation stimulates the mind to its highest possible function and amazingly, the skill to think outside of the box improves. You will find it normal to almost immediately see the great possibilities that will work with your ideas. Also, be reminded of this, you can only innovate if:

You are an independent soul and can break free from the crowd.
You fully understand and accept your responsibilities.
You have the power to make and keep commitments.

You do remember the three magic words, don't you?

Everything that happened was done because they were able to think outside of the box.

Read, Read, Read!

The experiences of the world can be found in books. Take time to locate a book that you find exciting and read, read, read. If you don't have a library card, go to your local library and get one. While there, browse and look for something of interest. Another resource is your local book store. Spend some time there and browse for something of interest. The library will offer many reading groups. Find one of interest and join.

I'm certain that every person in the world has a deep interest in something. Take your idea that is of deep interest to the library and search for a book of your choice. Appreciation, growth and innovation will come out of the experience.

Read, Read, Read!

Curiosity

Curiosity may kill a cat but it is critical toward a powerful mind. A topic in one of my classes one day was to consider the responsibility that business must play in maintaining our ecological system. I asked one young man what his thoughts were and his response was "who cares." Others went on with the topic and came up with some really good ideas. What is the difference between the student who said "who cares" vs those who became engaged? That word, of course, is *curiosity*. Those who are curious will dive into a challenge; those without curiosity will only touch upon it or leave it. For some, there is a natural laziness of the brain. Curiosity is the stimulus needed to kick-start the brain to create engagement with an idea. If there is no sense of focus, your accomplishments will be limited.

For those lacking a natural sense of curiosity, is there hope to create it? Yes there is, but it will take some special practice to develop. I was visiting an art museum with one of my young children and I noticed that he just kind of casually glanced at the paintings then went to the next thing. As we came to several Van Goh paintings, I noticed one where the storm clouds were very dark and ominous with an accompanying letter written by him to his brother.

I asked my son why he thought the storm clouds were so much darker than his other paintings. He studied several of the paintings, taking more time than usual, and commented that he couldn't guess. He then noticed the letter below the painting and began to read—soon reading in awe. The letter was the last letter written to his beloved brother and it read something like this "my dear brother, nobody knows better than you that the storm clouds have always been in my life, but now, they gather as never before." My son went back to gaze at the painting with the beautiful comment of WOW! What before was not interesting suddenly became interesting. Why? Because he took time to dig deeper. The goal here is to feed the appetite little-by-little.

A good place to begin is an art museum. Go online and locate the museum of your interest. Their websites will vary but you will find all kinds of interesting information. I jumped online at the Phoenix Art Museum and the painter Carlos Dolci caught my eye. Using a search engine, all the works of Dolci became available with his biography and information about his work. The paintings that caught my eye were worthy of intense study, so I used the Internet to learn more about their creation. It was exciting to know that I would soon be viewing that work at the Phoenix Art Museum. This is a process that can create a whole new world for you.

At the museum, study a painting and ask yourself many questions—what kind of a brush did the artist use to create the eaves on the house, how was he able to get the color and detail in the eyes so perfect, I don't see a line, yet I see an object, how could that be? Sculptures are amazing. Take much time and raise many questions about how things are created and ask questions of any museum associate nearby or discuss the work with your friend. If you find this exciting, develop the habit of visiting other museums in other cities and continue your excitement. If art is not your bag, there are all kinds of museums, such as planetary, science, business and industry, anthropology, etc. Even small communities will often have museum touting the history of the town and the area. Do it!

Attend a concert presenting classical music. Get a copy in advance of the program and choose any one musical selection, then go to the Internet and type the composer's name. You will get a ton of very interesting information. Read the biography and you will be amazed. Keep looking for ideas that will illuminate your understanding of the composer and why the work was done. Next, using the Internet, search the name of the composition you chose and you will again get much information.

Online, look for a copy of the work to purchase. Often times, you can find written material explaining the writing of the composition. This material may provide details about how certain passages were created and about recurring themes. Listen to the work and do so using the information you found, and continue this until you have come to understand and appreciate the work. Some parts may seem very beautiful to you and others uninteresting. The payoff will be when you go to the concert and hear the real thing. You will understand and enjoy it!

The whole idea is that you are digging much deeper into a subject until you gain some sense of understanding and appreciation. It works like giving a little boy candy, he will soon want more. In reality, you are learning to whet your appetite about something that never interested you before. There is something beautiful in everything, your job is to find it, learn about things and enjoy.

If you follow through with the ideas suggested here, please realize that this is only a start for you. Continue finding other things in which you might be interested and investigate in some detail. Soon, the candy is appreciated and you will seek more.

Do it!

Appreciation

You must continually stay on the positive side of thinking in order to stay mentally strong. In doing so, you will feel an increased sense of energy. Another tool available that will help keep you on the positive side, I call the *appreciation* tool. On Thanksgiving Day, I wrote a note on Facebook conveying a special idea to be grateful every day, not just on Thanksgiving Day. Begin each day with thinking through the many gifts that have been given to you—family, health, abundance, friends, etc. Then give thanks for all of these things. What a great way to start the day.

I'm sure there are parts of your life that are imperfect and there may be a thorn in your side, but don't let that take away the myriad of good stuff. While still lying in bed, think on the beauty of everything and your day will be improved.

A friend gave me this adage that I keep with me continually. The adage is, "if you cannot appreciate who you are or the things you now have, you will never appreciate who you could become or what you will get." There are many who go through life never satisfied, even though there is plenty. The adage holds absolutely true, give yourself and others your positive side.

Perspective

The idea of perspective is highly related to the ideas of awareness and appreciation, and serves the same purpose, that of stimulating the mind. The dictionary defines the word *perspective* as *view*. We believe that how one views the world is one's perspective. This is usually followed by the statement *reality for anyone is what one perceives*. I believe that this statement is true.

Two really important issues jump out at us regarding how people perceive (view) events. First, two people view the same event, yet each may provide a different explanation of what happened. How could this be? Another issue is the situation where a person has a change of heart from what they believed before. What caused the change?

To find an explanation for these two situations, let us compare one's perspective to a zoom camera. The camera can capture the entire broad scene of a yard or it can zoom in and display only the picture of a rose in the garden. Our perspective of things can be thought of as the mind, which may view an event from a broad view, being able to see all that was occurring, or another viewer who might be a young man who pays most of his attention to an attractive young lady in the scene–same picture, different view.

In cinematography, the usual approach is to take several shots of a particular scene. First, take a wide angle picture to display the total of all that is there. This provides an orientation and includes everything in the scene. The next shot will be an intermediate view showing interesting parts of the picture. This takes the viewer into a more detailed study of what is in the scene. The third shot will be a close-up that shows the details of the most interesting element in the picture. Viewers won't miss anything. That is, their prospective is broad and will include everything in the scene.

I believe that to be a complete thinker, we should always study the widest view of a situation, taking everything into consideration. Next, view and study several items that are of interest and thirdly, study in detail that in the scene which seems most important.

Historically, society tends to jump to conclusions on important issues. Television will broadcast the news of a crime and produce the mug shot of the offender that is quite unbecoming. For many, the jury is in, the man is guilty. One of the TV shows broadcast activities in the courtroom where much evidence is presented. Before a commercial break in the program, the commentator asked the viewers what the ruling should be. How ridiculous, only half of the evidence is in. Our system wrongly encourages us to make decisions before the complete picture is viewed.

The first skill to learn is how to take the wide angle shots and view all the information in the situation. Do not jump to conclusions. Narrow the view and gather more information, but continue narrowing to specific details that will provide the answer. William Deming, the noted TQM (Total Quality Management) specialist tells us that, "the answers are always found in the data, but the data must be complete and accurate." Developing this skill takes a special awareness, so please try to develop it as you face new problems.

The other skill needed is when you are facing a tough problem. The problem may be serious illness, financial problems, losing a job, or other critical things that can be debilitating to your ability to function. With any serious problem we naturally tend to get focused only on the zoomed-in picture. That provides quite a negative scene which of course generates a negative approach to solving anything. Because the problem is devastating, our perspective at this time is extremely narrow, yet the broader picture may produce the needed data for a solution. The problem seems to be the only thing in the world and tends to keep us in a narrow perspective. It is time to change that picture and it can only be done by expanding perspective.

My procedure was to put the problem at the center of a mediation session. While serving as the director of academic computing at our college, student usage was exploding and the operational budget was bare bones when our legislators decided to reduce funding for higher education. Soon after, a note appeared saying that our budget would be reduced by $80,000 for next year. Expecting a 25% student growth in our programs created what seemed to me an impossible situation and I was totally surprised and discouraged. We needed a miracle!

Later that day, I drove to a knoll overlooking a beautiful lake nearby. Meditation began in the usual way and I was able to let the problem go and my psyche received a great boost. At the proper time, I dropped the issue of the budget into the thought mix. There was no attempt to try and find an answer and the meditation continued for a time. Like a flash, the solution popped into my mind. Feeling quite certain about the solution, our group put the plan into action and we were able to recover the $80,000 from another source.

This worked because I was able to rid myself of the narrow perspective dragging me down and open to the widest possible perspective to find the solution. The solution was right in front of me. All I needed was to clear my mind from the negative disappointment to see it.

Life-Long Learning

Some of the great things about living in the USA are the opportunities available for every person in the country to improve their life. The many universities and technical schools have provided considerable opportunity, but now with the explosion of the community colleges, dreams to find a better way of life are all around us.

Community colleges offer the first two years of a bachelor degree serving as institutions right in your community with much reduced tuition rates. The relatively low cost makes it possible for students with less income to attend college.

Fifty years ago it was uncommon to see a 35-year old housewife whose children were grown start a college degree. Now it is quite common to see these same ladies enrolled at the community college and finish a bachelor or master degree at the university.

What so many people have not figured out is that community colleges also specialize in vocational programs that are amazingly successful. Glendale Community College in Glendale, Arizona has 60 vocational programs, many taking students to the highest levels possible. These programs include nursing, CAD drafting, computer graphic arts, photography, police and fire science, computer programming, computer systems management, computer maintenance, electronic manufacturing, automotive, business courses of all types, both for entry level and advanced level.

Professionals in many fields will take classes to update their skills either because of job requirements or the desire to improve. A 45-year old man showed up in my office at Glendale Community College for advisement. He was the head of the printing department at a large corporation. He failed to keep pace with the newer technology in graphic arts and when the office retooled to the new technology, it became clear that he could no longer hold his position and was released. He enrolled in a graphic arts program and worked seven to eight hours a day to gain the new skills. Within four months he was reemployed and enjoying a better life than before.

Many businesses have training programs that may be required or optional. Usually they are free and you don't need to travel far. How convenient is that?

The very strong point to make here is that *there are all kinds of systems in this country to help anyone improve life*. If you are in a position to need to grow or want to grow, get on the Internet and locate a place to satisfy your needs. It is out there.

Becoming and Staying Mentally Strong

Staying mentally strong is truly a responsibility that means so much to you, your family and your friends. Continued learning and growth will bring job advancement, better earnings and you enjoy your life and what you do. Being mentally strong means that you must decide to live in a positive world and develop great patience. Remember that self-improvement is a life-long process. Have a great life Captain!

Websites for Further Study

Mentally Strong

http://www.jongordon.com/blog/20-ways-to-get-mentally-tough-2/
http://www.inc.com/amy-morin/8-things-mentally-strong-people-do-every-single-day.html
http://www.wikihow.com/Stay-Mentally-Strong
http://www.affluentmagazine.com/articles/article/53
http://elitedaily.com/life/motivation/20-things-that-mentally-strong-people-dont-do/
http://www.huffingtonpost.com/2014/02/18/the-9-essential-qualitie_n_4760403.html

Curiosity

http://www.wellineux.com/articles/blog/mind/curiosity-life-giving-force
http://alyjuma.com/curiosity/
http://www.planetofsuccess.com/blog/2010/how-to-develop-curiosity/
http://ideas.time.com/2013/04/15/how-to-stimulate-curiosity/
https://experiencelife.com/article/the-power-of-curiosity/

Perspective

http://theincrementallife.com/7-tips-help-gain-new-perspective/
http://www.lifehack.org/articles/lifestyle/your-perception-is-your-reality.html
http://creativesomething.net/post/8215881557/why-you-need-to-broaden-your-perspective
http://blog.kevineikenberry.com/leadership-supervisory-skills/six-ways-to-expand-your-perspective/

CHAPTER SIX

Seeking a Spiritual Life

After telling a friend that I was going to include a chapter on being responsible for a spiritual life, his response was negative. His remark was "who do you think you are to be telling people they are irresponsible if they don't seek after God." In a sense, seeking a spiritual life is not in line with being financially responsible or taking responsibility for good health, as these things are pretty much accepted by society as the right thing to do. The spiritual thing is left for people as a choice, and that is the way it is presented here.

This chapter is written not on the basis of a responsibility but as a possibility. Finding my spirituality has reaped untold blessings and I give credit where it is due. My goal in this writing is to help people find a starting point for seeking after a spiritual life.

The idea of a spiritual life has many facets. Some see it as activities in a church, others as practices of the occult, yet others as the process of seeking an understanding of God. The discussion in this book relates to the two directions that I have experienced myself, seeking God through a process of meditation, and seeking God through an organized religion.

The human urge to seek some special power greater than ourselves has burned deeply in many cultures throughout history. We humans observe the marvel of the stars and planets, the flora and fauna, volcanos, etc. and feel that these things had to be created by a greater being than ourselves. Most of us ponder the eternal questions:

Where did I come from?
What is my reason for being?
Is there life after death?

All of these thoughts start us on the search for the answers to infinite questions.

Organized Religion

This portion of the book is written mainly for the person who has not begun a spiritual journey, but all are welcome to read these ideas. The first is the category of religion. A religious group usually consists of followers in an organized body of people who believe and follow a similar set of ideas. These ideas come from a highly spiritual enlightened person.

To paraphrase Deepak Chopra, he says that a new religion starts with a person who has experienced enlightenment regarding the great questions concerning our existence. Muhammad, the prophet, is considered the founder of Islam. Jesus Christ is the creator of Christianity. Brigham Young and Joseph Smith are the founders of the Church of Latter Day Saints, and there are many other examples.

As churches multiplied over the years, they tended to split into special groups. Thus we have the protestant religion having split off into Methodist, Lutheran, Presbyterian, Baptist, etc., and even subgroups created out of each one of these. The Catholic Church is huge and thrives in many parts of the world. There are many other religious institutions that have come into being in the recent past such as Christian Science, Religious Science, Unity, Scientology and others. The world now has a huge network of churches, many that might fit your needs.

What about finding my spirituality through organized religion? Okay, let's get started. The quickest and easiest way is to select a church in your immediate area and attend. You will use the Internet to help you find a church. Bring up your search engine (I use Google) and type in the phrase, *religious services near me.* You will find specific churches, mosques, and synagogues listed. Look until you find one in your area. Either select one of the institution's hotlinks or enter their name into the search engine and go directly to their website. Study that information and, if it suits you, note their worship times and attend a service. Continue your search until you find the one suited for you.

All churches usually claim to be friendly and caring. The truth is, some are, some are not. Some congregations will be made up of senior citizens, some of rich people, some of poor people, some with members of all ages. Some churches will have a ton of activities with organizations such as teen groups, retired people, young families, single people, men's groups, women's groups and the list goes on.

If you visit a church and are snubbed, don't be discouraged—obviously, that's not the church for you. We often give something a try and find it unsatisfactory, drawing the conclusion that all churches are lousy. Be patient and try and try again. It is a life-long commitment and will require some patience and persistence.

Once you find a church that you really like, study the opportunities offered and select one that you find most interesting. Go ahead and attend a session to see if it has something for you. One of my friends is a single lady and decided to attend the singles group in a particular church. Sadly, the experience was unfriendly, but she continued looking until she found the church where she felt comfortable. You will only get the best experience from a church by jumping in and becoming an integral part of it.

If you find a church and participate, you are on your way in your search for a spiritual life. I wish you every success.

Meditation and Prayer

If religious institutions fit the first category of spirituality, what is the second? Many people conduct their own search for spirituality through study, prayer and meditation. Prayer is thought of as *speaking* to God and meditation as *listening* to God.

In prayer, one must quiet the mind and focus on particular ideas. My prayers always start by giving thanks for the things given to me. If there is some pressing issue in my life, I ask for help in finding the solution. Some pray for healing both themselves and others. The prayer may be long or short, depending on the issues. Upon finishing your prayer, go directly into meditation.

Many spiritual seekers enjoy *meditation* as the pathway toward the discovery of infinite wisdom through God, but mediation is considered to be used in a variety of manners. Some use it for the purpose of creating strong positive feelings, others for improving health, some are able to control body functions such as pulse rate and blood pressure, some are able to experience revelation and some just enjoy the experience of full relaxation.

The major purpose, however, seems to be to connect to the hidden power that has created everything. We all spend much time where our conscious mind is in a constant chatter and we become unable to think outside of ourselves with so much busyness. The major goal in meditation is to still (quiet) the conscious mind, eventually enabling the mind to reach beyond itself and make the connection with the infinite power. In doing this, one can open communication with the infinite mind. Many of your most perplexing problems will point to solutions through revelation.

I'm sure that most of you have experienced the situation where the solution to a problem or some special revelation comes to you, seemingly, from out of the blue. My goodness, where did that come from? We generally call this *intuition*. This often happens when you have forgotten about the problem to be solved. Quieting the conscious mind and going deeper into meditation fosters these kinds of events. There are many people who attribute their personal success to following their intuition. Remember the single, most important goal is to connect the mind to the infinite power of God. This will require special dedication.

I encourage you to kick-start your search for spirituality, for it may open doors never before dreamed. In doing so, the best place to start is using the Internet. Using a search engine, type *meditation*. Don't be confused by the massive amount of information, just pick and choose what seems interesting to you from the choices. For example, the Wikipedia article on Meditation is a good overview, covering a number of religious perspectives. As you read and study, you will end up narrowing the categories until you find one to embrace. Once you narrow to a specific methodology, look for a good book on that subject and let it become your guide.

A usual question from beginners is, "When will I know that meditation is working for me?" There are varying levels of success and you will progress through them. How much time it takes depends much on your ability to focus and how often you meditate. In the beginning, you will become an expert on developing the ability to relax. That will be a great benefit and will likely come first.

The difficult part is to be able to release the every-day chatter from your mind. This will be difficult at first, but keep trying and you will gradually be able to still the mind. Once the mind is clear after prayer, it is open to receive revelations from the higher source of our creation. The Guru that helped me learn meditation told me to simply release random thoughts as they pop into my mind. While meditating a thought will pop into your head, acknowledge the idea then simply say "I release you," and continue meditating. After a bit, you will experience longer periods of nothingness in your mind. The time needed for meditation varies considerably. My morning and evening prayer and meditation are usually short, 20 minutes to 30 minutes. Meditating to look for a problem solution varies from 10 minutes to 2 hours.

There will be times when a thought or inspiration comes into your mind quite unexpectedly. If you feel that the thought is truly coming as an inspiration, digest it and apply it as necessary. Intuition usually comes to me with a strong note of confidence and I know it is the proper solution. Other times nothing may come. In either case, close with a prayer of thanksgiving. Even if you received no intuitive message, the experience of the meditation is extremely calming and peaceful.

The question arises during meditating, how do I tell the difference between an ordinary thought and intuition? An ordinary thought will always be related to many ordinary things that concern you, such as: what will I cook for dinner? When is Jim's birthday? I have a dental appointment on Friday. Intuition will catch you by surprise, it will be unrelated to your daily chores, and you will recognize it as important.

I will always meditate when a serious problem arises in my life. The process here is to do my usual prayer and meditation. Toward the end of the meditation I simply state the problem mentally and wait. You dare not consider the possible solutions for, in doing so, you would be giving control of your thoughts back to the conscious mind thus abandoning the higher state of mind. Just introduce the problem and wait quietly. Sometimes a solution comes immediately, other times a day later, sometimes no answer. Just try again.

In meditation, you will be on a life-long journey. You will experience many unexpected benefits and your life will be better. You will be pursuing the questions that the greatest of people in our history have sought. It is a life-long commitment and will require much patience.

You may be concerned with the question, *"How will I know that I am doing what's right for me?"* No one can answer that question except you. Certain things will touch your mind in a special way, so you go in that direction. The truth is that you are on a life-long journey. All seekers will become enlightened in different ways at different times, and you will not likely find absolute perfection while on this earth. The other truth is that, in your journey, you come closer and closer to your utopia.

You will come across good meditation books in your Internet research. If you find a title that touches you in a special way, buy it. A major source of materials used in my meditational studies is written by Dr. Wayne Dyer. He has written widely and is quite concise in his presentations. Give him a try.

As for me, I regularly attend a Christian church and am active in their work. I really enjoy the lessons, the music, and the comradery. I also use prayer and meditation every day to fully maintain my spirituality. For me, life becomes more beautiful every day because of it.

God speed, on your journey Captain.

Websites to Help in Your Spiritual Journey

http://goodlifezen.com/how-to-embark-on-a-spiritual-journey/
http://www.schoolofspirituality.org/Pages/Drops.htm?gclid=Cj0KEQjw57W9BRDM9_a-
http://zenhabits.net/meditation-guide/
http://www.gty.org/resources/questions/QA121/what-should-i-look-for-when-choosing-a-new-church-home
http://www.findachurch.com/a_hme/hme_hme.asp
http://www.islamicfinder.org/
http://www.myjewishlearning.com/article/find-a-synagogue/